THE ART OF KATE GREENAWAY

A NOSTALGIC PORTRAIT OF CHILDHOOD

INA TAYLOR

For Alice Victoria

Title page:
Kate's favourite apple tree features in this illustration from her 1888 book the PIED PIPER OF HAMELIN *(see page 90).*

First published in Great Britain in 1991 by
Webb & Bower (Publishers) Limited,
5 Cathedral Close, Exeter, Devon, EX1 1EZ

Distributed by the Penguin Group
Penguin Books Ltd, Registered Offices: Harmondsworth, Middlesex, England
Penguin Books Australia Ltd, Ringwood, Victoria, Australia
Penguin Books Canada Ltd, 2801 John Street, Markham, Ontario, Canada L3R 1B4
Penguin Books (NZ) Ltd, 182–190 Wairau Road, Auckland 10, New Zealand

Designed by Peter Wrigley

British Library Cataloguing in Publication Data

Taylor, Ina
The art of Kate Greenaway: a nostalgic portrait of childhood.
1. English illustrations. Greenaway, Kate, 1846–1901
I. Title
741.942

ISBN 0–86350–397–7

Text is set in Fournier

Typeset in Great Britain by P&M Typesetting Limited

Colour and mono reproduction by Mandarin Offset

Printed and bound in Hong Kong

THE ART OF
KATE GREENAWAY

'AFTERNOON TEA' in the best traditions of the Aesthetic movement with sunflowers, Morris-style rush-bottomed chairs and blue and white china.

CONTENTS

"THE GIRL'S OWN PAPER."] EDMUND EVANS, PRINTER. [LONDON.

A SPECIMEN PAGE OF MISS KATE GREENAWAY'S WORK.

From the "Pied Piper of Hamelin." (F. Warne & Co.)

Introduction

There was a time when meadow, grove, and stream,
The earth, and every common sight,
To me did seem
Apparelled in celestial light,
The glory and the freshness of a dream…
Heaven lies about us in our infancy!

'Intimations of Immortality
From Recollections of Early Childhood'
William Wordsworth

Opposite:
A Greenaway interpretation of Utopia, the land where the Pied Piper ultimately led the children.

NO OTHER BOOK ILLUSTRATOR has achieved the fame of Kate Greenaway, a fame which has continued unabated for more than a century, as strongly in the Far East as in Europe. Throughout this time her books have remained in print and her illustrations used to decorate various objects. To many people she represents not a person but a style, almost a cult. Kate Greenaway's art conjures up an imaginary world where children dance in flowery meadows and nursery rhyme characters find a life which is forever beautiful and innocent.

In the Greenaway world it is nearly always May and the early summer sun is encouraging the apple and hawthorn to blossom. Children are tempted out of doors to play, wearing their new sprigged muslin frocks and summer bonnets. Older sisters take afternoon tea in formal gardens where Nature has been thoroughly tamed. Geraniums and lilies bloom in geometrically shaped beds contained by neat box hedges and gravel paths; the trees are a model of the topiarist's art, and roses fastened to white trellising scent the air. There is beauty in order and security; nothing is allowed to run wild and threaten the tranquillity.

Much of the attraction of the Greenaway world lies in its lack of realism. We know that children grow up and roses have thorns but most of us cherish a deep-seated nostalgia for what might have been. If only life were as innocent or as beautiful as in her nursery books. It jolts us then to discover that many of the landscapes and cottages in Kate's romantic pictures really existed and were sometimes sketched from life. A study of her unfinished Memoirs reveals for the first time that Kate Greenaway's art was far more firmly rooted in reality than anyone has suspected. Episodes from her own childhood appear in her books; favourite places and people turn out to have been the inspiration for illustrations. The elaborate dresses and large decorated hats worn by the little girls in her paintings were actually designed and stitched by the artist herself, to be worn by her child models in the cause of authenticity. Even the regimented garden had a real-life original, carefully memorized by Kate and used as the basis for her pictures and the layout of her

Ride a cock-horse,
To Banbury-cross,
To see little Johnny
Get on a white horse.
K.G
33
D

Above:
Twin-gabled houses appear in the background of many of Kate's pictures and were also esteemed by devotees of the Aesthetic movement.

Opposite:
To Kate's mind there was nothing more delightful than an old green gate to enclose a cottage garden and later in life she ensured her own house at Hampstead had exactly that.

Home-Beauty.

"MINE be a cot," for the hours of play,
Of the kind that is built by Miss Greenaway,
Where the walls are low, and the roofs are red,
And the birds are gay in the blue o'erhead;
And the dear little figures, in frocks and frills,
Go roaming about at their own sweet wills,
And play with the pups, and reprove the calves,
And do nought in the world (but Work) by halves,
From "Hunt the Slipper" and "Riddle-me-ree"
To watching the cat in the apple-tree.

O Art of the Household! Men may prate
Of their ways "intense" and Italianate,—
They may soar on their wings of sense, and float
To the au delà and the dim remote,—
Till the last sun sink in the last-lit West,
'Tis the Art at the Door that will please the best;
To the end of Time 'twill be still the same,
For the Earth first laughed when the children came!

AUSTIN DOBSON.

PUSSY CAT, PUSSY CAT.

Pussy Cat, Pussy Cat, where have you been ?
I've been to London to look at the Queen.
Pussy Cat, Pussy Cat, what did you there ?
I frighten'd a little mouse under the chair.

Kate Greenaway appears to have been anticipating Beatrix Potter by a few years in this unusual illustration where an animal is dressed as a human.

Right:
Kate Greenaway at her best, handling the delicate subject of a mother and her child.

Opposite:
Kate worked these beautiful designs of little children around a poem by Austin Dobson. The end result was published in the MAGAZINE OF ART *in 1883.*

own garden at Hampstead. To understand Kate Greenaway's early life is to understand her art, for she virtually painted her autobiography.

What also emerges from her unpublished writings is Kate's great love of flowers. At times her studio resembled a florist's shop, abounding with flowers in boxes and vases, some purchased by herself, others sent by friends. The blooms not only gave her pleasure but also served as models for her drawings. Only in recent years has Kate Greenaway's skill as a flower painter been more widely recognized, though her contemporary, the cottage artist Helen Allingham, remarked that no one could paint a rose like Kate.

It is strange to think that Kate Greenaway was truly a Victorian, born in the middle of the nineteenth century and dying the same year as the Queen. Her simplicity of line and delicacy of colour seem far removed from the heavy ornate style we associate with Victoriana. Kate's rise as a book illustrator came at a time when childhood was regarded as a symbol of lost innocence, babies as earthly angels 'trailing clouds of glory'. Much mawkish

Right:
*This watercolour of '*LITTLE POLLY FLINDERS*' was painted by Kate for one of her later books,* THE APRIL BABY'S BOOK OF TUNES, *published by Macmillan.*

Opposite:
The background in this picture of 1881 owes much to Kate's childhood memories of Rolleston. The round hayricks were in Mr Chappell's farmyard and the peacock and round bird house in the garden of the Neale family, who lived opposite the church.

sentiment accompanied this Victorian cult of childhood, but on the one hand it did remove children from the horrors of mines and factories and on the other inspired some exquisite nursery art.

Three important children's illustrators emerged in the 1870s, producing books of genuine artistic merit: Walter Crane, Randolph Caldecott and Kate Greenaway. These artists raised the status of nursery art for the first time and demonstrated the potential that the medium had for developing fantasy themes impossible in adult art. Whether the beautiful books they produced were designed more for adults than children has been much debated. Artistically conscious Victorian parents welcomed the books warmly as playing a valuable role in educating the taste of their offspring. Strangely, although the books illustrated by the two men enjoyed much popularity at the time, they have not endured as well as those by Greenaway.

Kate can claim the dubious honour of being the first person to see her work extensively reproduced for sale. Had she chosen, she could have decorated her home with 'Kate Greenaway' figurines and wallpaper, taken tea from crockery bearing her illustrations, dressed in 'Greenaway' frocks from Liberty's London or Paris stores and purchased a host of ephemera crudely plagiarizing her art.

The widespread use of Kate's designs around the world continues as strongly today, showing how timeless are the illustrations of this Victorian woman. Part of the charm lies in the essential Englishness of her style. Although her subjects at times verge on the sentimental, her work never cloys, for it is tempered with gentle humour. At the end of the twentieth century, what we appreciate most about the art of Kate Greenaway is its inherent simplicity and lightness of touch.

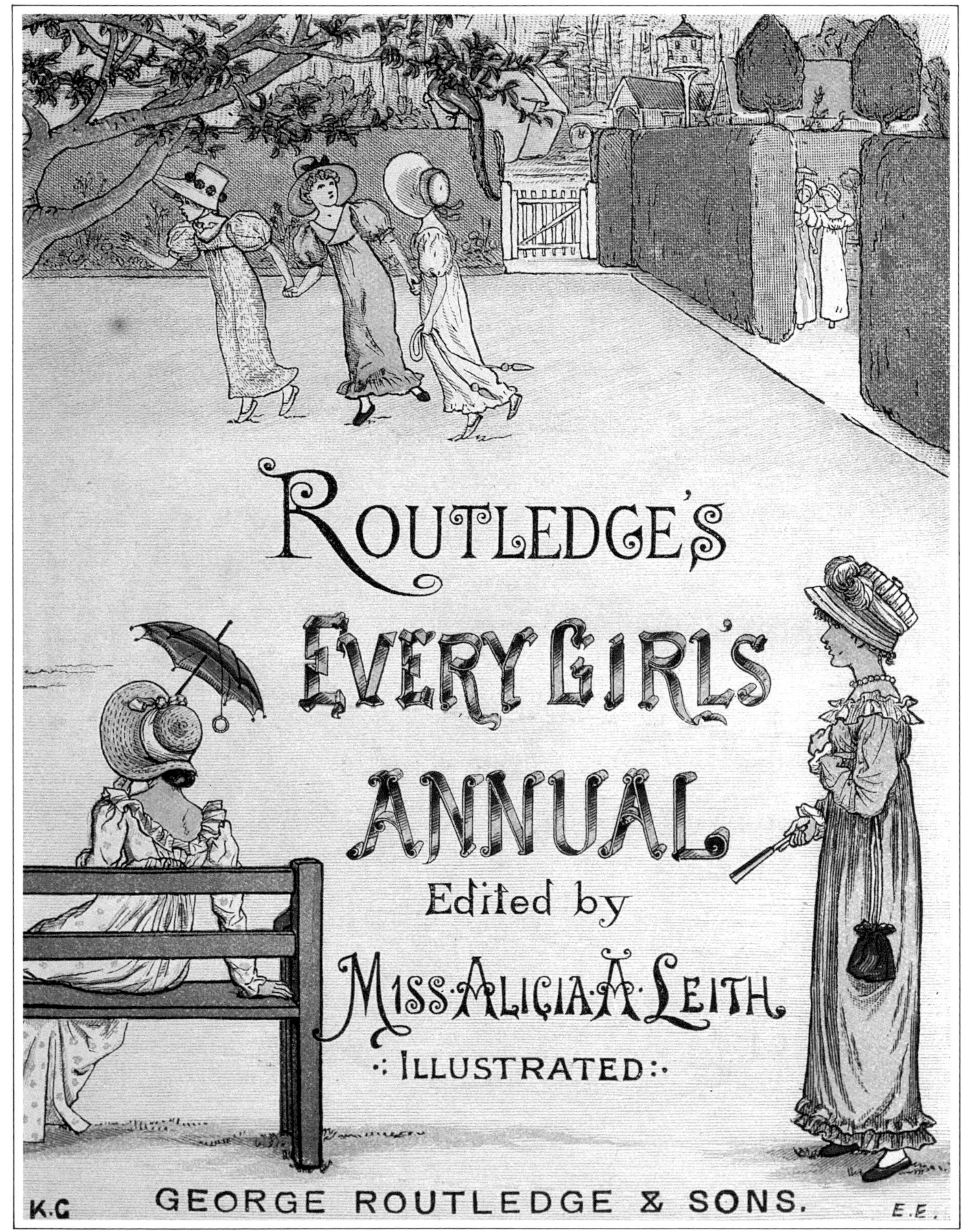
ROUTLEDGE'S
EVERY GIRL'S
ANNUAL
Edited by
MISS·ALICIA·A·LEITH
·:·ILLUSTRATED·:·
K.G
GEORGE ROUTLEDGE & SONS.
E.E.

1

THE CHILD

Opposite:
Whilst having no difficulty depicting beautiful young women and children, Kate was the first to admit that backgrounds and foregrounds presented her with major problems.

Despite her enormous fame and the entrée into society which she gained later in life, Kate Greenaway was adamant that childhood was her happiest time and that she had never wanted to leave it. In contrast with most girls, she recalled hating growing up and crying when forced to wear her first long dress.

So attached was she to childhood that she never married, living virtually all her life with her parents and brother. Made to accept adult status by the time she was twenty, Kate returned to her youth in her art. Her paintings and book illustrations depict the real and imaginary world inhabited by Kate Greenaway between 1846 and 1866. Since she possessed an extraordinary photographic memory, the actual clothes, colours, dreams and landscapes she had once known reappear on paper. Although J M Barrie's famous play *Peter Pan* was not produced until after her death, Kate Greenaway could almost have been a model for it, the girl who would not grow up. John Ruskin, the art critic, was fascinated by this aspect of her personality, telling the thirty-nine-year-old artist: 'You are a mixed child and woman and therefore extremely puzzling to me.'[1]

It is surprising that Kate should have thought her childhood so idyllic, for she was not a spoilt only child, nor yet the baby of a large family, simply the second of four children. She herself admitted it was curious that she found life so much happier than her brother and sisters did, in exactly the same surroundings. 'I suppose my imaginary life made me one long continuous joy – filled everything with a strange wonder and beauty ... the golden spectacles were very very big'.[2]

In fact by the time Kate was born, on 17 March 1846 in Hoxton, north London, Greenaway family life was far from golden. The financial situation had reached crisis point. Her father, a freelance master engraver, had recently completed a commission to engrave all the wood blocks for the printing of an illustrated book when the publisher announced he could not pay: the firm was bankrupt. Money was always tight in the family at the best of times because John was expected to contribute to the upkeep of his widowed mother and two unmarried sisters as well as support his wife and children. Things were not made any easier by John Greenaway being a gentle unworldly sort of person, who adored children and animals and would have been perfectly content to spend his time sketching. It was the knowledge of how precarious the painter's life could be which had caused his mother to direct him into engraving and arrange his apprenticeship with Ebenezer Landells in Fleet Street, one of the leading engraving firms in the capital. There his fellow apprentices had been Myles Birket Foster, later to become an important watercolour artist, and Edmund Evans, who went on to develop a technique of colour printing which brought him fame as the printer of books by Walter Crane and Randolph Caldecott, and most of all by Kate Greenaway. Compared with the rise of his colleagues, John Greenaway's career proceeded fitfully.

It has often been assumed John Greenaway was the person who most inspired Kate. Certainly, from an early age she could be seen with her pencil and slate trying to imitate her father. She also took after him in looks and temperament. It was, however, her mother who shaped the nature of Kate's art.

Elizabeth Catherine Greenaway (née Jones), with her dark hair and dark eyes, was recognized as a beauty, with a striking resemblance to portraits of Mrs Siddons, the actress. She was a spirited individual who, as a young girl, had rebelled against the tight lacing and stiff whalebone corseting she was forced into 'to mould her figure'. In protest she cut the laces and designed and made her own clothes. The young Miss Jones's dresses sound similar to those later favoured by the Pre-Raphaelite women, for they wore loose flowing garments in shades of green and blue. Her needlework was so exquisite that she was soon requested to make elaborate pin-tucked frocks for her mother and frilly hemmed shirts for her father. Talented though she undoubtedly was at designing and stitching clothes, Elizabeth had to understand that she could have no career, but would have to marry and use her skill to amuse herself and clothe her family. Indeed Kate wore clothes made by her mother during most of her life.

When the family fell on hard times, Mrs Greenaway considered

Kate liked nature to be firmly under control, so the roses appear fastened to lattice trellising in the background to this delicate study of a mother with her children.

"O, come, pretty fairies,
And live in our house;
Come bird and come bee,
And come little field-mouse:
Come blue dragon-fly,
And come butterfly bright;
And bring all the friends
You would care to invite!"
"There are pantries and dairies
Convenient for fairies–
A ball-room to dance in,
A court-yard to prance in–"

One of Kate's early greetings card designs for the Belfast firm of Marcus Ward (see Chapter 2).

Right:
The tree which cradles 'HUSH A BYE BABY' is a flowering apple tree. This and the hawthorn were Kate's favourites because of the wonderful contrast between the gnarled old branches and the delicate flowers.

Below:
An early pencil study of children at the beach. The little girls in this picture are clad in contemporary costume rather than characteristic Greenaway frocks.

A study of drapery which is of a similar style to the May Queen's dress Kate designed for Whitelands College, Chelsea (see page 120).

what she could do to help. Initially she was too weak from Kate's birth to do more than accede to her husband's request to take five-year-old Lizzie and baby Kate with her to Nottinghamshire to be cared for by her wealthier relatives. In their absence, John Greenaway moved to cheaper lodgings and sought more work. When she felt stronger Mrs Greenaway determined to take a more active part in extracting the family from the financial mire. Thinking of her skill as a dressmaker, she persuaded her husband to rent different lodgings in neighbouring Islington. Opposite the church she had discovered a large but dilapidated Elizabethan house divided into three shop units with living accommodation behind and above. Sandwiched between an ironmonger's and a brush shop, Mrs Greenaway opened her first shop selling children's clothes she made herself and fancy trimmings such as lace, feathers and ribbons.

The family lived there only three years, early in Kate's life. Nevertheless, she retained some vivid memories of the building's crumbling grandeur and all her life had a preference for old buildings. Black and white timber-framed mansions appear in the background of some of her book illustrations.

Mrs Greenaway possessed far more business acumen than her husband and whilst he struggled on, obtaining intermittent commissions for books and periodicals, she supported the family financially. Her children's outfits were so popular she could not

Right:
Kate's love of timber-framed houses dated back to the early years she spent in part of a crumbling Elizabethan mansion in Islington.

As she tells us in her Memoirs, Kate drew many of her children's party illustrations from memories of events she had attended as a child in Islington.

keep pace with demand and had to take on outworkers. At the same time she sought larger premises which would enable her to expand into ladies' millinery, another field she was adept at creating items for. In the summer of 1852, when Kate was six, Mrs Greenaway moved further up the same street to a larger shop at the fashionable end of Upper Street, Islington, and since the new premises were a lock-up, the family lived in a house down one of the alleyways behind. Now occupying a prime position, Mrs Greenaway's business flourished. Her rise can be seen in the way she variously described her occupation over the years. Initially she decided she was a milliner but by the 1860s she thought 'lace shopkeeper' more appropriate; a few years later it was 'dealer in underclothing', rising eventually to 'ladies' outfitter' – the ultimate title.

As the business grew, so did the number of assistants and outworkers, which enabled Mrs Greenaway to spend a little more time with her growing family. In July 1852 she gave birth to her fourth and last child, Alfred John, known as Johnny. He joined the three Greenaway girls, eleven-year-old Lizzie, six-year-old Kate and two-year-old Fanny. Kate gained more pleasure from her baby brother than her sisters did, for to her Johnny was a real-life doll who could be dressed up and paraded around the street. She took great interest in the many outfits her mother stitched for him. Even at the end of her life Kate could recall exactly what feathers had been used to trim a particular white leghorn hat or what shade of green velvet the rosette on his little jacket had been. Johnny Greenaway's baby clothes were to reappear in many of his sister's pictures.

The family spent twenty years living at the smart end of Islington and Kate stored away memories of life there. What she enjoyed most were the frequent parties held for the shopkeepers' children. Recollections of these formed the basis of her later pictures of little boys and girls dressed in their best party outfits, complete

Opposite:
The model for 'THE FLOWER GIRL' was a watercress seller Kate saw in Islington.

SCHOOL BOARD
FOR LONDON
SECOND SCHOOLBOARD
HOU

The frontispiece to a book about amateur dramatics.

Right:
The background to the picture is Rolleston, where the River Greet flows through dykes edged with pollarded willows and bullrushes on its way to join the River Trent.

Opposite, above:
The influence of paintings by Gainsborough and Romney, as well as memories of clothes from her childhood, are evident in Kate's preliminary work for her painting 'GIRL WITH A BLUE SASH'.

Opposite, below:
The faces peering over the wall have a nightmarish quality which appears in several pieces of Kate's early work. The characters here are based on villagers from Rolleston.

with lace handkerchiefs and fans, self-consciously trying to ape their elders. Kate could remember in minute detail what clothes the children had worn. The three Greenaway girls themselves were dressed modestly by contrast. They always wore the same white muslin frocks to parties, changing only the sashes to blue, pink or white. Long black lace mittens were an essential accessory. None of this impressed their more prosperous neighbours. 'We were undoubtedly looked down upon, we were not smartly dressed or at any rate not to their taste', Kate reminisced; '– we didn't have a smart house, we didn't do anything that would have drawn their respect upon us'.[3]

Ironically, by the turn of the century when the Greenaway cult was at its peak, such frocks were regarded as the height of children's fashion and available from the new Liberty's store in Regent Street, London.

Kate remembered that when she was young the children of the butcher and tobacconist were invited to far more parties than the little Greenaways, but she was unconcerned. All she wanted was to be permitted to go and view the party-goers, resplendent in their outfits, before they left for the festivities. From an early age she became the quiet observer, storing away in her memory images of the children's clothes and behaviour. At the same time she absorbed ideas from patterns and fabrics which she saw in her mother's shop. She was forever begging offcuts of material to make up garments for her dolls, which she was devoted to.

City life was exciting for young Kate. She liked the flamboyance of the street entertainers, the decorations in shop windows and the bands she went to hear with her father. Nothing, however, matched her pleasure in her other life in Nottinghamshire.

Every year from babyhood until her early twenties, Kate spent four or five months of the summer in a small village. There could hardly have been a greater contrast between London and Rolleston,

Little maid, little maid,
Whither goest thou?
Down in the meadow
To milk my cow.
KG
41

Relying on her memories of milking at the Chappell's smallholding in Nottinghamshire, Kate created this picture for her book MOTHER GOOSE.

Kate's memories of Phyllis Chappell and her sister Ann rick-building at their Rolleston farm were the inspiration for this charming scene.

five miles outside Newark close to the Lincolnshire border. It only boasted two hundred and fifty souls, most of whom eked out a humble farming existence. Mrs Sarah Aldridge, Mrs Greenaway's sister, was at the upper end of the village hierarchy since her husband farmed over two hundred acres, employed a dozen labourers and retained a family pew in the church.

However, Kate rarely stayed with these relations. Dating back to the time when she had been brought to Rolleston as an infant and nursed in the village, she remained firmly attached to the Chappell family. Phyllis Chappell, in her late fifties, was regarded by the Aldridges as an old family retainer, since she had spent years in service with them. So when Mrs Greenaway had arrived exhausted with an infant and young child, the baby had been hastily weaned and passed to Mrs Chappell for care whilst Mrs Aldridge coped with her sister and the older child.

Kate believed she spent virtually all the first two years of her life with the Chappells. So attached to them did she become that she called them Mamam and Dadad and, Mrs Chappell's spinster sister Ann, Nanan. These names, like her affection for them, lasted until the end of their lives.

The Chappells were smallholders, owning three cows which they grazed on the common land so they could use their fifteen acres near the cottage for winter fodder. Kate was able to watch haymaking in the fields behind the farmyard and ride home on the top of the haywagon ready to see the rick building in the yard. Every morning she asked to be woken early by Ann so that she could go and fetch the cows for milking. Later in the week she would stand in the cool dairy and study butter making as Mrs Chappell churned and squeezed and patted. Unwittingly, Mrs Chappell and Ann became the forerunners of many a winsome dairy maid in Kate's nursery books.

Mr Chappell was by the time Kate knew him 'a poor creature'; even his own wife said that. Somewhat feeble-minded, he was unable to contribute much to the running of the smallholding, but propped up the gate and waylaid likely passers-by in conversation. The presence of a child animated him and he managed to make a small wooden hayfork and milking pail so that Kate could help Ann with the chores.

The pace of life at Rolleston was slow and though it was the middle of the nineteenth century, little had changed in fifty years. Mr Chappell favoured a brown fustian smock just as he had decades earlier as a wagoner's lad. Mrs Chappell and Ann still wore bonnets from earlier days with borders around the face, which necessitated careful washing and quilling (curling) of the ribbons. Kate had only seen such things in old-fashioned prints; they were never stocked in her mother's shop.

Whilst the fabrics and dresses she saw in London supplied ideas for the foreground of her artwork, Rolleston provided the pastoral inspiration. Though Kate was essentially a Londoner, she regarded Rolleston as her spiritual home and liked to boast that she had had a country upbringing. Because it was always summer time when she stayed, it is usually summer in Kate's pictures. Those wintry scenes she was later obliged to draw for almanacs and Christmas cards were executed with the greatest reluctance and based on town scenes. For preference Kate would set her pictures in the month of May, the time she usually arrived to stay with the Chappells at Rolleston, when the hedgerows and meadows were breaking into bloom.

An informal sketch Kate made to amuse one of the daughters of Edmund Evans, the printer with whom she was later to be associated.

The furnishings in the Chappells' cottage were old hand-me-downs and a source of wonder and inspiration to Kate. The room she always slept in contained a four-poster bed with chintz hangings and the country chairs were rush-bottomed. This

When Kate stayed with the Chappell family as a young girl, she was always given the four-poster bed to sleep in. She could remember the furnishings in that room in minute detail and they are reproduced from memory here.

furniture was to be drawn many times over the years. Downstairs stood an old grandfather clock, which Mr Chappell ritually opened and wound up by hauling on the chain. In the parlour was a dark oak corner-cupboard filled with old china, left to Mrs Chappell by an elderly aunt. On a rainy day, or a Sabbath afternoon when work was forbidden, Kate would be allowed to examine these pieces. The two-handled posset cup once used for christenings and the blue and white china bowls all appear on dressers and tables in the background of her pictures. She knew their designs off by heart, but by then she also owned the originals, left after the Chappells' death to the little girl who had admired them most.

Better than handling the china, Kate loved to be permitted to open the oak chest in Mrs Chappell's bedroom. This was a treasure trove of old clothes. There were old shawls and cloaks, muslin frocks and quilted silk petticoats jumbled up with snippets of ribbon and lace. Also in Mrs Chappell's bedroom was a wonderful patchwork counterpane which had been made from remnants of hundreds of worn-out garments. Kate was transfixed by the old fabrics, whose colours and patterns she thought prettier than anything she had ever seen. Once again she stored the information away.

It was at Rolleston that Kate first came to appreciate flowers and gardens. A walk across the fields behind the Chappells' farm early in the summer would cover her shoes with a gold dust from the pollen of masses of cowslips, Kate remembered. It was 'a sort of Eden – or Paradise – where the air was scented with apple blossom and you walked through cowslips or seemed to live in a sea of buttercups and daisies that were everywhere – a world covered with flowers and blue sky and divinely fresh air.'[4] The flower-strewn Rolleston fields appear again and again in Kate's art.

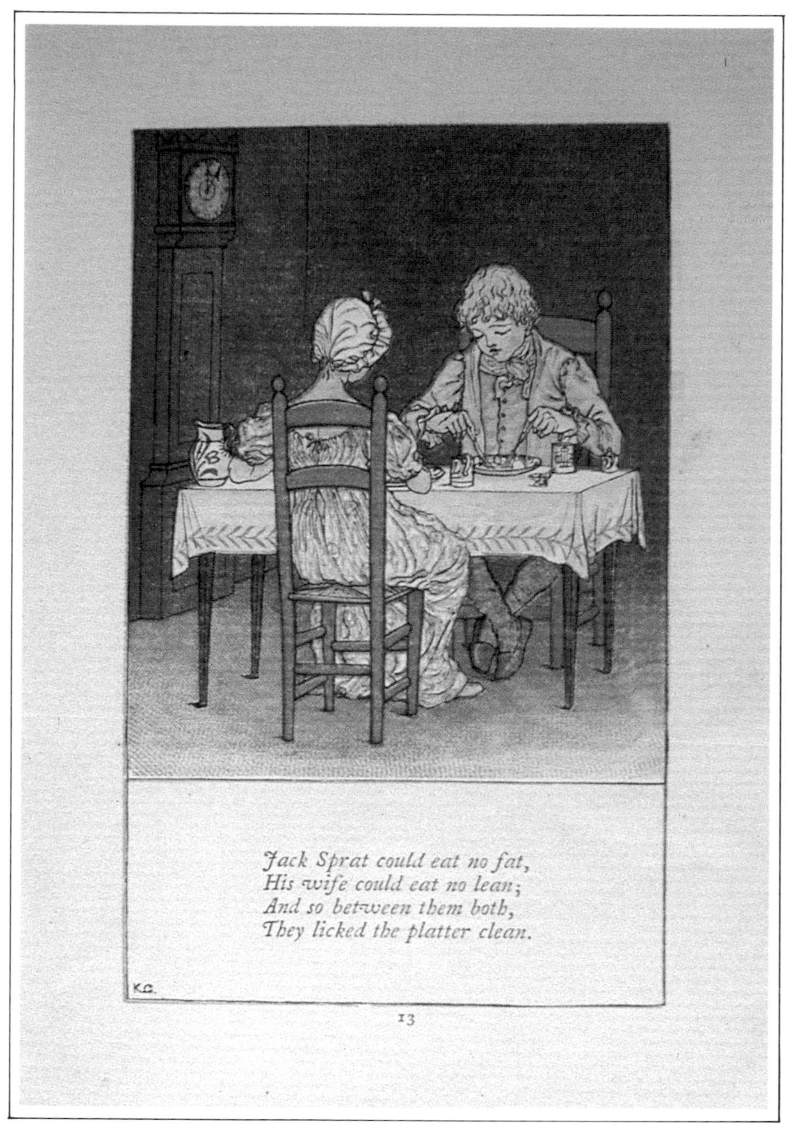

Jack Sprat could eat no fat,
His wife could eat no lean;
And so between them both,
They licked the platter clean.

Mr and Mrs J Sprat seen dining at the Chappell's farmhouse. Kate became well acquainted with the grandfather clock, rush-bottomed chairs and blue and white china on her annual visits.

Mary, Mary, quite contrary,
How does your garden grow?
With silver bells, and cockle shells,
And cowslips all of a row.
KG
26

In Kate's ideal garden everything was tamed and trained. Her paintings were often based on memories of the Neales' garden at Rolleston. It is interesting to compare this 1881 picture with the later one on page 28 (right).

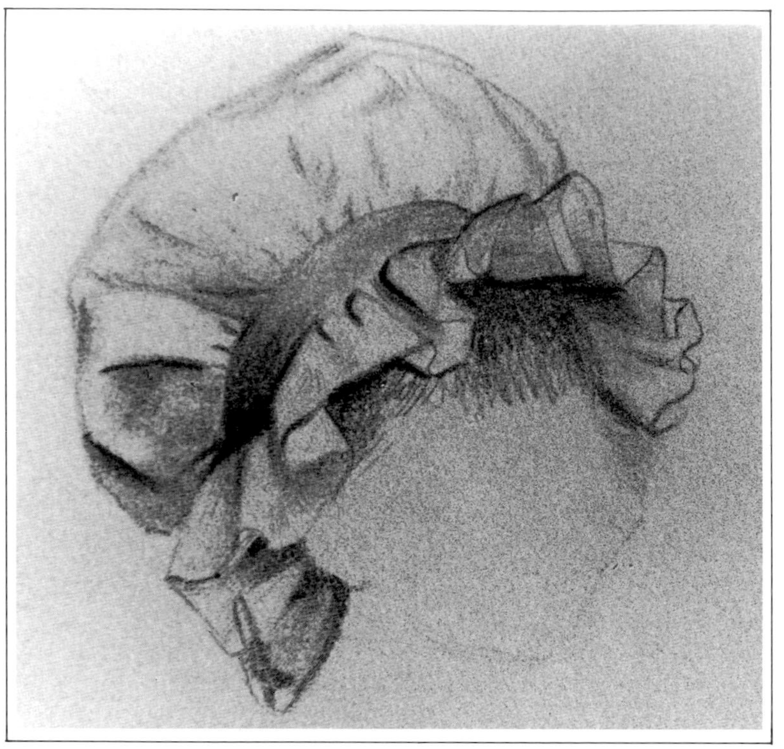

MARY, MARY, QUITE CONTRARY.
Mary, Mary, quite contrary,
How does your garden grow?
With silver bells and cockle shells,
And pretty maids all of a row.

The nursery rhyme 'MARY, MARY, QUITE CONTRARY' gave Kate the perfect excuse to indulge in one of her regimented gardens. This picture appeared in her 1900 book THE APRIL BABY'S BOOK OF TUNES.

Above, left:
A study for one of the famous Greenaway mob caps.

Left:
'JACK AND JILL', based on Kate's nephew Eddie and her favourite model Mary, climb up a daisy-strewn hillside such as Kate loved in her childhood.

The cottage next door to the Chappells had a wall smothered in old-fashioned rambling roses. On her way to fetch the cows with Ann at five-thirty in the morning, Kate found the scent from this rose heavenly. She always maintained that once she smelt a flower it would immediately suggest to her a hundred different scenes far away from where she was. Roses were a lifelong delight to her and drawn not only for their own sakes but woven into borders to frame sketches.

The colours and scents in the cottage gardens at Rolleston pleased her, but at the same time these self-same gardens offended her innate love of order. Nature rampant, burgeoning over hedgerows and round cottage doors, appalled her. Kate liked her plants firmly under control: bordered, clipped, trained and contained. She never possessed a garden in Islington, for the Greenaways' house had only a yard behind it. Occasionally when she played in a side street, she would peep through the gates of a big house and choose a garden she wished was hers. In Rolleston Kate was often taken by Mrs Chappell on visits, some of them to the Neale family, who had also once employed Mrs Chappell. They had a large old house opposite the church which, according to Kate, contained 'my loved one of all gardens I have ever known'.[5] Towards the end of her life Kate began writing down stories of her early memories and when she came to this garden, she dwelt on it for several pages. She could recall the shapes of the flowerbeds as well as how they were planted. From her description of the gravel paths passing between neat oval beds bounded by box hedges and of walled gardens and espaliered trees, the inspiration for her garden pictures and the design of her own garden at Hampstead is immediately obvious.

Her summer experiences in the Nottinghamshire countryside, combined with the love of clothes and fabrics she inherited from her mother, formed the basis of the unique Greenaway style.

REFERENCES

1 Letter from John Ruskin to Kate Greenaway Jan 1885
2 Letter from Kate Greenaway to Violet Dickinson 29 Nov 1896
3 Memoirs
4 Ibid
5 Ibid

Kate adored the scent of old-fashioned roses which reminded her of the cottage gardens in Nottinghamshire. To her delight she later encountered similar roses in John Ruskin's garden at Brantwood.

No. 5.
A SONG OF A DOLL.
Con espressione.
1. I once had a sweet lit - tle doll, dears, The

2

Art Schooling and Early Career

Opposite:
The garden in the background of this charming scene epitomizes everything Kate admired – gravel paths edging neat flowerbeds, trellis fencing and topiary.

KATE'S EDUCATION was rather haphazard. In later life she was to regret this as it left her with a poor command of the written language. Letters to important people in the art world or society cost her much agonizing because she knew her grasp of punctuation and spelling to be shaky.

Her schooling began and ended with three weeks at a dame school learning her letters. She could recall Mrs Allaman, the teacher, sitting with a big alphabet book on her lap and a child standing by her side reciting. Drawing from memory later on, Kate used just such a vignette to begin the illustrations for a spelling book. In addition to reading, the infants made a start on sewing in preparation for embroidering some God-fearing sampler. Kate's enthusiasm for stitching led her to jab the needle into the teacher's finger accidentally and she was admonished with a sharp tap on the head from a silver-thimbled finger. That signalled the end of her formal schooling.

Although her mother tried Kate, together with one of her sisters, at several different schools, she either became very distressed or developed a psychosomatic illness which forced her to stay home. Finally Mrs Greenaway relented and employed Miss Daisy to teach all the Greenaway girls at home three afternoons a week. As was frequently the case, such 'teachers' were simply women who had fallen on hard times and sought a respectable way of earning a living. With no opportunity for further education, these women rarely had much learning to impart. Miss Daisy's credentials were that she could play the piano and had a French mother. Thus for years the children learned little but French and music. Kate claimed that she had avoided even these subjects and spent most of her time sketching. But she did acquire a sufficiently good grasp of French to be able to read books in that language when she was older.

Mrs Greenaway's experience of life convinced her that all her children, girls included, should possess some skill which would earn them a living if necessary. Kate's elder sister Lizzie profited from Miss Daisy's lessons, becoming competent enough at the piano to

Drawn by Kate and engraved by John Greenaway, this illustration was published in the book THE CHILDREN OF THE PARSONAGE *in 1874.*

Above, left:
Once again, Rolleston was the inspiration for this ink drawing (with deliberately reversed initials) Kate prepared for a magazine.

Left:
These three pencil studies are most likely to be of Kate's nephew, Eddie Dadd, son of her younger sister Fanny.

attend the Royal Academy of Music and study the instrument under William Sterndale Bennett. She later went on to work as a music teacher until she married in her mid-thirties. It was felt Kate too needed a skill which could support her for, as the family admitted, she was distinctly odd. They found it difficult to imagine the quiet girl, who passed much of her time in a fantasy world, ever leaving home to marry and have children of her own. With her talent for drawing and her father's contacts in the publishing world, a future in commercial art seemed most appropriate.

John Greenaway had recovered sufficiently from his earlier business difficulties to employ three assistants and receive regular work from *The Illustrated London News.* As a master-engraver he frequently took on an apprentice. Whilst it was inconceivable for a girl to be apprenticed, she could nevertheless learn to be an engraver's assistant and find work in the growing periodicals market. Kate's sixteen-year-old cousin Marian Thorne, who came to live with the Greenaways after her father's death, was learning wood engraving from Mr Greenaway. It seemed likely Kate would follow suit or, better still, learn to illustrate designs for him to cut. In order to improve Marian's drawing abilities, she was sent to evening classes twice a week at the nearby Finsbury School of Art. Kate, though only twelve years old, was also enrolled so she could chaperone Miss Thorne during the mile walk to school.

Surprisingly, it was Marian who disliked the formal lessons and Kate who thrived on them. Although the elder girl gave up attending, Kate pleaded to be allowed to continue and was transferred to the daytime sessions. The Finsbury School of Art was a branch of the Central School of Art in South Kensington and the brainchild of Henry Cole who wanted to encourage art-craftsmen rather than pure painters. During her six years there, Kate learned much about creating patterns for ceramics, textiles and architectural ornaments. She followed the National Course of Art Instruction which was well suited to someone who possessed exceptional colour awareness and had already shown interest in fabric designs. Having found work she enjoyed, Kate became a conscientious

The influence of Rossetti, whose art Kate admired greatly, can be seen in this early wood cut. It was a design for a book called THE FAIRY SPINNER *published in 1875.*

student, receiving several prizes during the course, culminating in a bronze medal in a national competition in 1864 for six tile designs.

At nineteen, having successfully completed all the stages of the National Course, Kate moved to the Central School in South Kensington. Like the Royal Academy Schools this supposedly offered women the best art training available, but many believed it was still inferior to that offered the men, since females were not permitted to draw from the nude or even the draped model. This ensured their figure drawing was permanently at a disadvantage. Some determined women students set modesty aside and attended one of the more liberal evening classes. Kate went first to Heatherleys to draw from life and the costumed model but did not like the informal teaching method, so when the Slade School opened in Gower Street in 1871, advertising equal opportunities for men and women, she enrolled in their evening classes. With fellow students Evelyn De Morgan, Mary Kingsley and Helen Allingham, Kate studied under the inspired direction of Edward Poynter.

Although she now attended both day and evening classes, these were not full time and, like other students, she was able to prepare for exhibitions and take on commercial work. The one place all young artists hoped their work would be shown at was the Dudley Gallery in Piccadilly. Opened in 1866, this gallery had become recognized as a nursery ground for rising artists. Consequently, academicians, members of the two established watercolour societies and publishers frequented the Dudley to talent spot. Kate's first exhibits in 1868 were two works, a watercolour called 'Kilmeny', which was her interpretation of a folk story, and a set of six line drawings in one frame. The latter were intended for drawing on to wood blocks and subsequent engraving. The thorough understanding of this medium which Kate had gained from her father ensured her work sold easily at two guineas.

The line drawings were bought by Mr Loftie, editor of the *People Magazine*, and later published in his journal with the addition of stories and verses. Three of the drawings were scenes in a child's life and the others fairy subjects.

Above, centre:
This study for an early painting called 'THE DAISY CHAIN' shows clearly how Kate began work with a pencil outline and then filled in the detail of the figure afterwards.

Above, left:
A study of Mary, Kate's favourite model, whom she drew from the age of around seven until her early twenties.

Above, right:
Although the girl in this early Greenaway picture is dressed in contemporary costume, she has the large eyes and characteristic heart-shaped face of Kate's later girls.

Kate's illustration entitled 'INEXHAUSTIBLE PURSE' is from FAIRY GIFTS, *a very early book to which she contributed illustrations. The name of the engraver, Kate's father, is seen in the left-hand corner.*

These were not the first of her illustrations Kate saw in print, for in 1867, when she was twenty-one, her work appeared as the frontispiece to a book called *Infant Amusements* which offered 'practical hints to parents and nurses on the moral and physical training of children'. The commission had been secured through her father, then engraving blocks for another book from the same publisher, Griffith & Farran.

The high quality of John Greenaway's work, along with his contacts in the publishing world, were a great asset to Kate, ensuring that many small commissions for children's book illustration came her way over the next few years. Equally, her association with W J Loftie proved useful, leading her into another expanding field, the greetings card. This was still restricted mainly to Christmas and Valentine cards, but the firm of Marcus Ward and Company in Belfast had plans to extend their range with more artistic works in bright colours. Their overtures to William Loftie led to Kate receiving commissions for many cards, beginning in 1868.

Identifying early Greenaway greetings cards is not easy since Kate rarely signed her work and neither she nor Marcus Ward kept any precise records or samples. The colours used are not those readily associated with Kate Greenaway for there was much use of gold and bold colours. Only the children's clothing gives a hint of the artist. It did not take the publishers long to realize their young artist was especially talented at drawing costume; subsequent greetings cards amply demonstrate this.

In order to get the detail correct, Kate went to the London art galleries and museums to study costumes of specific periods. Flowing medieval robes appeared on the Valentine cards in 'The Quiver of Love' series and sumptuous eighteenth-century hats and dresses were used for a range of Christmas and New Year cards. These latter cards, entitled 'Youth of Sir Joshua's Day', were based on Kate's first-hand study of Reynolds portraits. She admired his work greatly as she did the other eighteenth-century masters, Gainsborough and Romney, and made regular pilgrimages to the

It is interesting to compare Kate's original pencil ideas (left) for this illustration with the final printed version (right).

The girl with the badminton racket was considered a very versatile design by Marcus Ward and Company who issued it variously as a Valentine, Christmas, New Year and, as here, general greetings card.

National Portrait Gallery to study their paintings. The details of costume and pose she observed there greatly influenced her art.

As the daughter of a dress designer, seamstress and milliner, Kate found no difficulty in translating what she saw in a picture into a real garment. The costumes she required were cut out and stitched, not always full-size but to fit either a large doll or her lay figure (artist's poseable figure). This enabled Kate to draw from life and get the exact light and folds. So talented was she at this sort of needlework that friends would request her help in making fancy dress or artistic clothing for their offspring. Sadly, none of these original Greenaway garments has survived; it is likely Kate herself unpicked and remodelled most of them once they had served their purpose for, like many Victorians, she was thrifty.

Illustrations for greetings cards continued alongside those for books throughout the 1870s. The circulation of some of Marcus Ward's cards was phenomenal. One of Kate's designs, for which she was paid a flat rate of three pounds, sold over 25,000 copies within a matter of weeks. Others, like 'The Quiver of Love' and 'Melcomb Manor', proved so successful as a series of cards that they were reissued in gift-book form. Although the cards brought in poor return for the amount of effort required, they did have the merit of putting her work in the public eye which in turn helped her to gain commissions from periodicals. After the popular children's magazine *Little Folks* began to use Miss Greenaway's line drawings in 1876, others followed suit, and not just in England. Through the publisher Frederick Warne and his agency with the American children's magazine *St Nicholas*, Kate's illustrations appeared on the other side of the Atlantic the following year.

Opposite, above:
Kate's New Year card was in a series called 'GOOD OLD TIMES' and produced by the Belfast firm of Marcus Ward.

Opposite, below:
This boldly coloured picture entitled 'THE COURSE OF LOVE' was originally used on a greetings card in 1874. Marcus Ward and Company decided to republish it the following year in a gift book called MELCOMB MANOR.

POOR little maid,
quite vexed indeed,
She stops to speak,
he pays no heed;
Yet seems she fair
and winning too;
Ah friend-the blame
must lie with you!
My NEW YEAR greeting, love & kiss
To you he bears, then tell me this:-
What must he look in you to find
Who leaves so sweet a maid behind?
MARCUS WARD & CO.

THE COURSE OF LOVE.
How smooth these gentle waters are
Beneath the summer's glow.
Alas, that Love, more gentle far,
So smoothly may not flow!

MORE THAN KIN,

These two greetings cards produced in 1880 were part of a series of four entitled 'YOUTH OF SIR JOSHUA'S DAY' and demonstrate the influence of Reynolds on Kate's work.

Below, left:
The influence of Gainsborough is clearly seen in the costume of this girl from Kate's 1884 book LANGUAGE OF FLOWERS.

Quaking-Grass . *Agitation.*
Quamoclit . . *Busybody.*
Queen's Rocket . . . *You are the queen of coquettes. Fashion.*
Quince . . . . . *Temptation.*

35

Above, right:
This charming study was also inspired by the Gainsborough paintings Kate saw on her regular expeditions to London art galleries.

PSALMS AND ANTHEMS

TO BE SUNG AT THE

Anniversary Meeting

OF THE

CHARITY CHILDREN

IN THE

CATHEDRAL CHURCH OF ST. PAUL,

ON THURSDAY, JUNE 7, 1877;

WHEN A SERMON WILL BE PREACHED BY

THE RIGHT REVEREND THE LORD BISHOP OF MANCHESTER

Before PRAYERS the 100th Psalm.

ALL people that on earth do dwell,
Sing to the LORD with cheerful voice:
Him serve with fear, His praise forth tell,
Come ye before Him, and rejoice.

The LORD, ye know, is GOD indeed;
Without our aid He did us make:
We are His flock, He doth us feed,
And for His sheep He doth us take.

O enter then His gates with praise,
Approach with joy His courts unto:
Praise, laud, and bless His name always,
For it is seemly so to do.

For why? the LORD our GOD is good,
His mercy is for ever sure:
His truth at all times firmly stood,
And shall from age to age endure.

THE PSALMS FOR THE DAY

TO BE CHANTED BY THE GENTLEMEN OF THE CHOIR, THE CHILDREN TO JOIN IN THE GLORIA PATRI TO EACH PSALM.

AFTER THE FIRST LESSON,

TE DEUM (*Goss*),

BY THE GENTLEMEN OF THE CHOIR AND THE CHILDREN.

AFTER THE SECOND LESSON,

JUBILATE DEO (*Goss*),

BY THE GENTLEMEN OF THE CHOIR AND THE CHILDREN.

BEFORE THE PRAYER FOR THE QUEEN,

THE CORONATION ANTHEM,

BY THE GENTLEMEN OF THE CHOIR; THE CHILDREN TO JOIN IN THOSE PARTS OF THE GRAND CHORUS WHICH ARE PRINTED IN ITALICS.

ZADOK the priest, and Nathan the prophet, anointed Solomon King.
And all the people rejoiced and said: *God save the King, Long live the King, God save the King, May the King live for ever, Amen, Amen, Hallelujah, Hallelujah, Amen.* *God save the King, Long live the King, May the King* … *May the King live for ever, for ever, for ever. Amen.*

Opposite, above left:
Part of Kate's original programme for the Charity Children's Anniversary Meeting at St Paul's on 7 June 1877, with her lightning sketches in the margin.

Opposite, above right and below:
The procession of Charity girls drawn by Kate at the St Paul's service. The pictures were published in an American children's magazine called ST NICHOLAS.

Above:
A rare Kate Greenaway seaside study from one of her sketchbooks.

Right:
Kate was fascinated by drapery and able to reproduce it well, as this pencil study shows.

Kate's favourite round bird house makes an appearance as early as 1876 on this design for the Valentine gift book THE QUIVER OF LOVE.

An unusual medieval scene drawn by Kate Greenaway for use as a greetings card and later published in THE QUIVER OF LOVE.

3

THE BREAKTHROUGH

Edmund Evans photographed in the early 1880s. His technique of colour printing from wood blocks raised the level of nursery-book production to an art form.

Some time during 1877 John Greenaway wrote to his old colleague Edmund Evans, by then a successful colour printer with his own premises in Racquet Court off Fleet Street. Greenaway believed that if Kate's drawings had any commercial merit, Evans could be the one to recognize it. Out of this initial overture came an invitation for Greenaway and his daughter to visit the Evanses at their home in Witley, Surrey, adjacent to the Birket Fosters.

The small dark-haired woman who arrived by train from London with her father could hardly have differed further from Evans's expectations. Despite earning her living in the male-dominated graphic art world, Miss Greenaway was anything but an emancipated young woman. Instead Evans was introduced to a dowdy matronly figure who was shy, lisped like a child and seemed desperately anxious to please.

Kate was frightened of Edmund Evans, as she was of most men. This was not helped by information she had gleaned about his strict Quakerism; one of the first things she noticed on arrival at Leybourne, the Elizabethan-style mansion he had built, was the scriptural text carved over the front porch. Kate also knew that Evans possessed the power to make her as famous a children's book illustrator as Walter Crane and Randolph Caldecott, whose nursery books he engraved and printed.

What Kate showed Edmund Evans was a portfolio of some fifty drawings with accompanying verses. She was apprehensive about subjecting them to criticism by a third party because they were based predominantly on her favourite scenes and experiences at Rolleston. The tea-parties which formed such an important part of village social life were depicted; Kate's favourite garden at Rolleston with its formal flowerbeds edged with box hedges and gravel paths appeared in several pictures; the Chappells' water pump, hayricks and geese were all there, as were the pieces of old china Mrs Chappell kept in her parlour. From her city childhood memories, Kate drew the forerunner of the pushchair, a little cart with a string attached in which she had once been obliged to drag

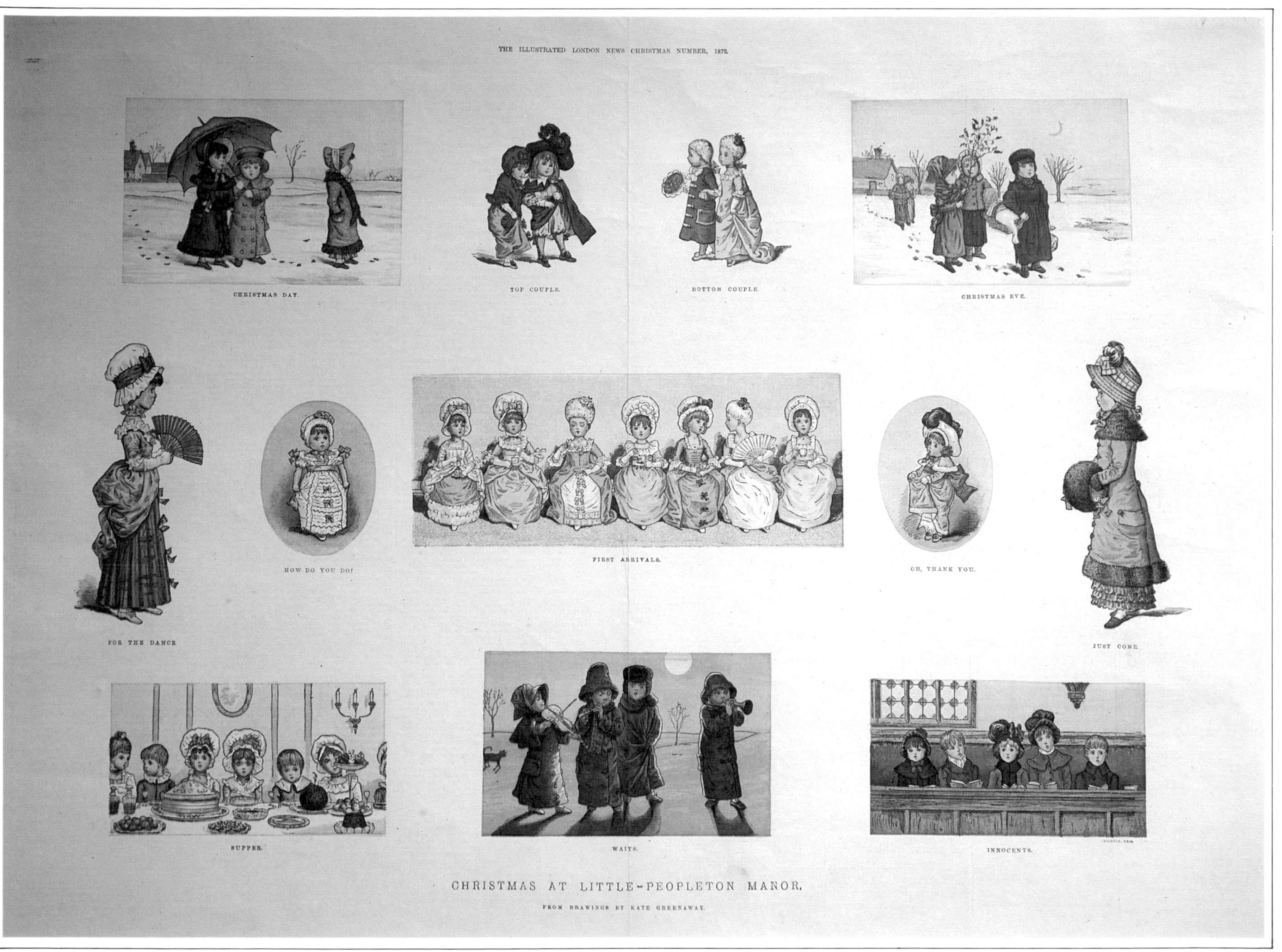
THE ILLUSTRATED LONDON NEWS CHRISTMAS NUMBER, 1879.

CHRISTMAS DAY.

TOP COUPLE.

BOTTOM COUPLE.

CHRISTMAS EVE.

FOR THE DANCE.

HOW DO YOU DO?

FIRST ARRIVALS.

OH, THANK YOU.

JUST COME.

SUPPER.

WAITS.

INNOCENTS.

CHRISTMAS AT LITTLE-PEOPLETON MANOR.

FROM DRAWINGS BY KATE GREENAWAY.

These drawings of 'CHRISTMAS AT LITTLE PEOPLETON MANOR' appeared in the Christmas edition of the THE ILLUSTRATED LONDON NEWS *the same year as Kate's first book was published.*

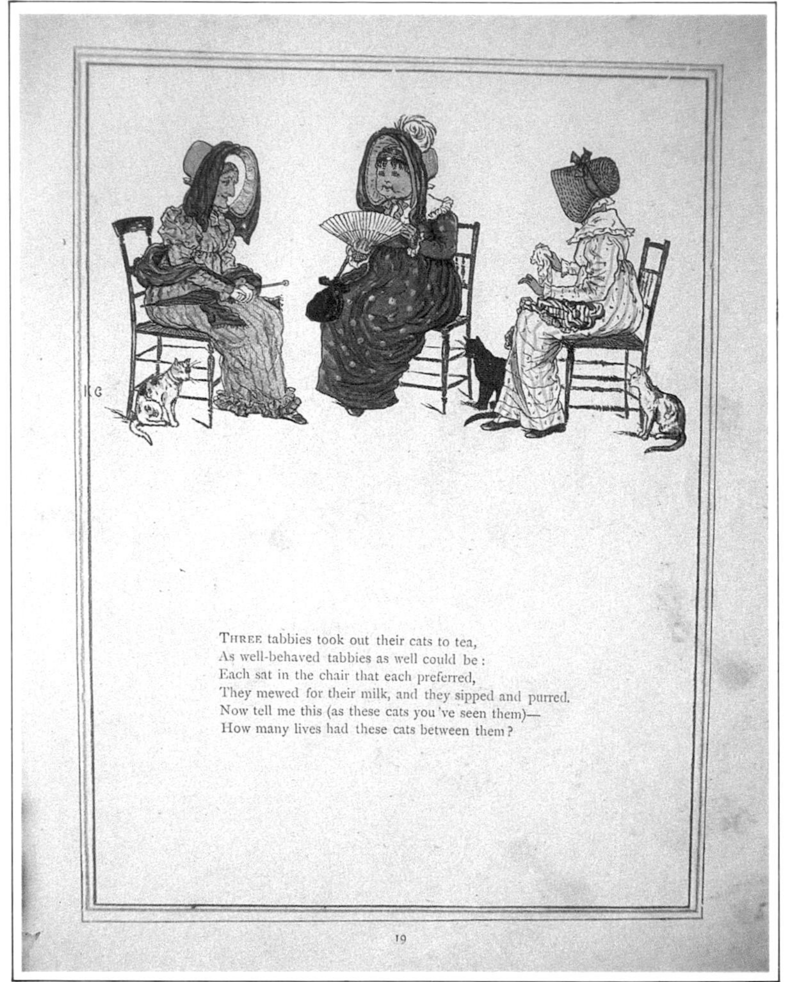

THREE tabbies took out their cats to tea,
As well-behaved tabbies as well could be:
Each sat in the chair that each preferred,
They mewed for their milk, and they sipped and purred.
Now tell me this (as these cats you've seen them)—
How many lives had these cats between them?

19

The three matrons taking tea with their cats are an amusing interpretation of the tea-parties Kate attended in Rolleston with Mrs Chappell.

This illustration is based on Kate's own memories of having to drag her baby brother Johnny round in his 'chaise', as the family called it. The little cart, sometimes pulled on a string, turns up in several of her pictures.

Opposite:
Kate's excellent sense of layout enabled her to design books in their entirety, right down to the contents page.

Below:
To many, sunflowers epitomized the Aesthetic movement. Kate later grew them in her garden at Hampstead from seeds she brought back from Ruskin's home in the Lake District.

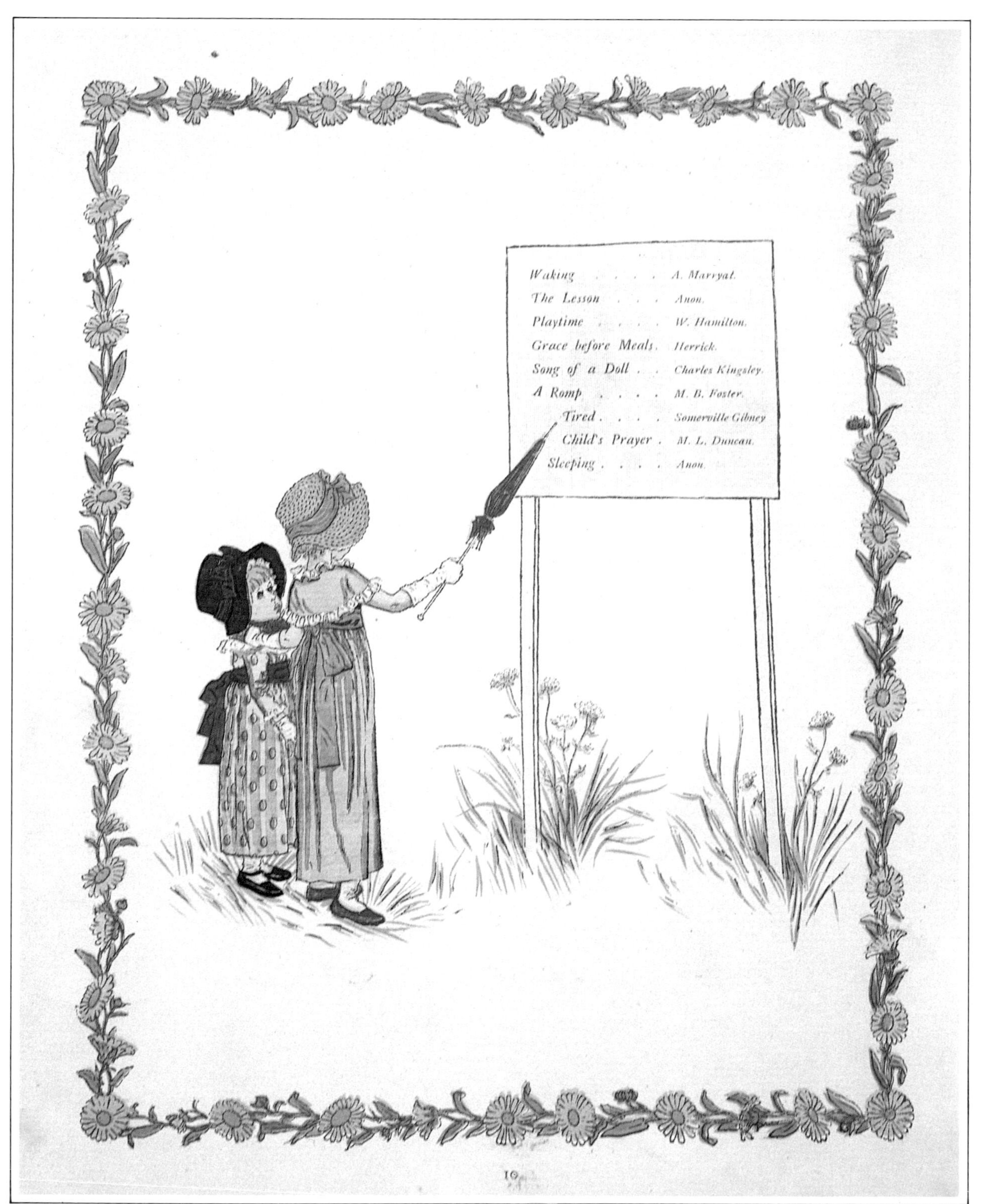
Waking . . . . A. Marryat.
The Lesson . . . Anon.
Playtime . . . . W. Hamilton.
Grace before Meals. Herrick.
Song of a Doll . . Charles Kingsley.
A Romp . . . . M. B. Foster.
Tired . . . . Somerville Gibney
Child's Prayer . M. L. Duncan.
Sleeping . . . . Anon.

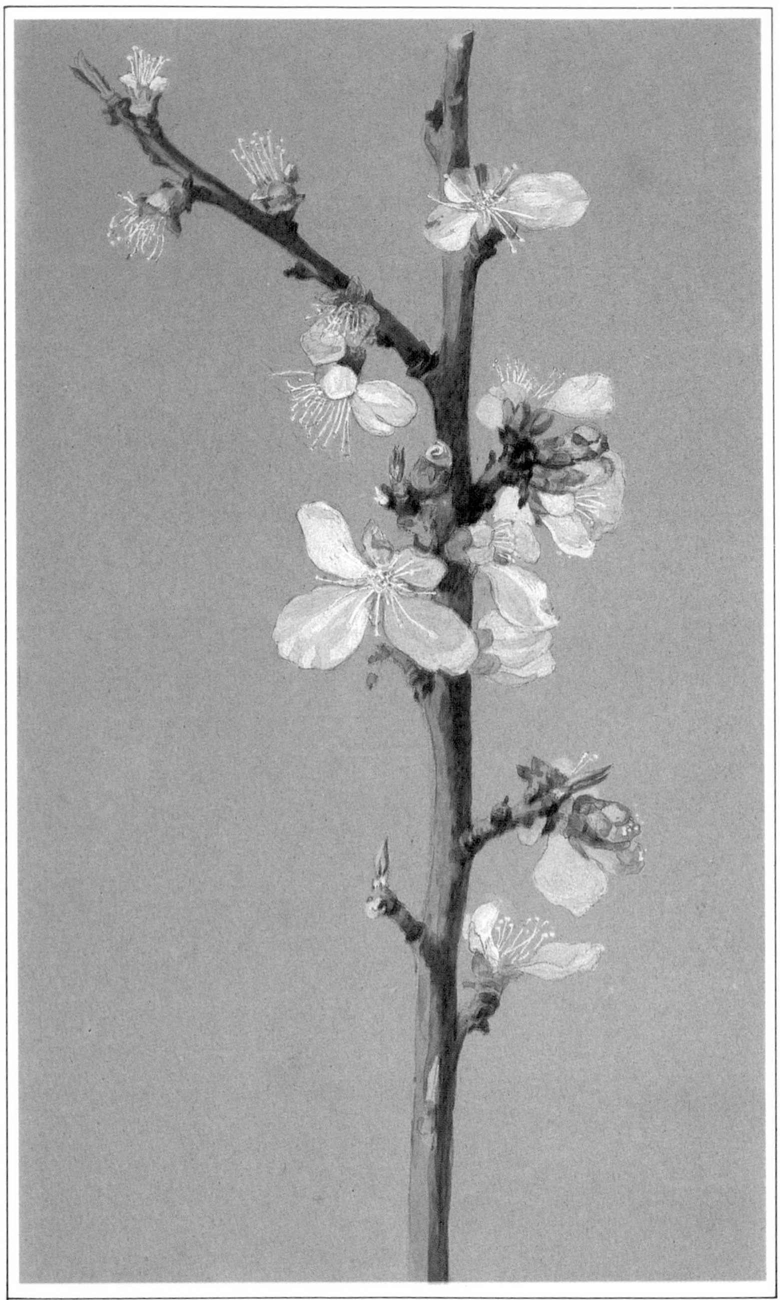

her baby brother round. In another picture appeared a recurrent dream she had of a secret garden ablaze with nasturtiums, hidden high up among the London roofs and chimney pots, which could only be reached by magically stepping over the tiles. In the foreground of these pictures were children costumed in beautiful print dresses and hats from an earlier age.

Evans was unaware of the source of Kate's imagination but was astounded that her watercolours bore all the hallmarks of high fashion. Kate's maidens wore loose dresses in the much-satirized 'greenery-yallery' colour; they sat on William-Morris-type rush-bottomed chairs, drank tea from the blue and white china which Rossetti had brought into vogue and danced in gardens planted with sunflowers and Japanese-style flowering trees. All embodied perfectly the spirit of the new Aesthetic movement.

Evans realized that Kate's clean unfussy lines and pure colours were ideally suited to his method of wood-block reproduction. It was evident she had a good sense of layout: each of the fifty sheets was bordered and contained a verse and illustration elegantly set out. He had no doubt that here was potentially a beautiful children's book. What he did have reservations about was her poetry which struck him as little better than childish doggerel. Quite apart from the errors of spelling and grammar, the lines were often so contorted so as to secure the necessary rhyming couplets that they made nonsense.

At first Evans tried to persuade Kate to sell her drawings without the verses, but he soon discovered there was more mettle in this quiet woman than he had imagined: 'I should say she was decidedly a strong-minded woman', he wrote towards the end of his life.[7] Kate's dealings with Marcus Ward and Company, who had bought her original artwork for a pittance and thereafter reproduced it in various guises without paying another penny, had taught her a lesson. Sensing she held the trump card this time, she refused to let her illustrations appear without the verses, even though she suspected her poetic gifts to be limited – Marcus Ward had once dismissed her verses as 'rubbish and without any poetic feeling'.2 A compromise between Edmund Evans and Kate Greenaway was finally reached, whereby her verses could appear, subject to a poet friend of Evans correcting 'a few oddities'. Kate won the day but had to accept Evans's outright purchase of her original artwork; he in return agreed to pay her a third of the profits from the book's sales, rather than the more usual one-off payment. Both sides were happy, and armed with what he was convinced would be a success, Edmund Evans approached his friend George Routledge to publish *Under The Window*.

The apprehension Kate felt on first meeting Edmund Evans gradually vanished, to be replaced by a rewarding personal and professional friendship. Far from being a sombre religious type, Evans was extremely sociable and possessed an infectious sense of humour. Kate found he shared her love of the countryside and was himself fond of taking his watercolour box out to paint from nature. His wife Polly, niece of Birket Foster, also became a good friend; she was far younger than her husband, indeed much the same age as Kate. The five Evans children too were great favourites with the artist and the inspiration for many sketches; even the family's home, Leybourne, was drawn, and substituted for one of the houses in that first book.

Kate was captivated by the Surrey countryside, as many artists before her had been. Encouraged by the Evanses' overwhelming hospitality, she began visiting regularly. Her holidays in Nottinghamshire declined with Aunt Aldridge's move from the county and the death of various members of the Chappell family. Surrey conveniently fulfilled Kate's yearning for a country retreat and had the advantage of being only a short railway journey from London. The cottages and farms which appear in the background of some of her pictures can often be identified as those near Witley. What Evans also offered Kate were new friends and contacts in the art world. At Witley she met Randolph Caldecott, on a visit to his publisher, and she resumed acquaintance with her former art school friend, Helen Allingham, then making regular summer visits to paint the old Surrey cottages.

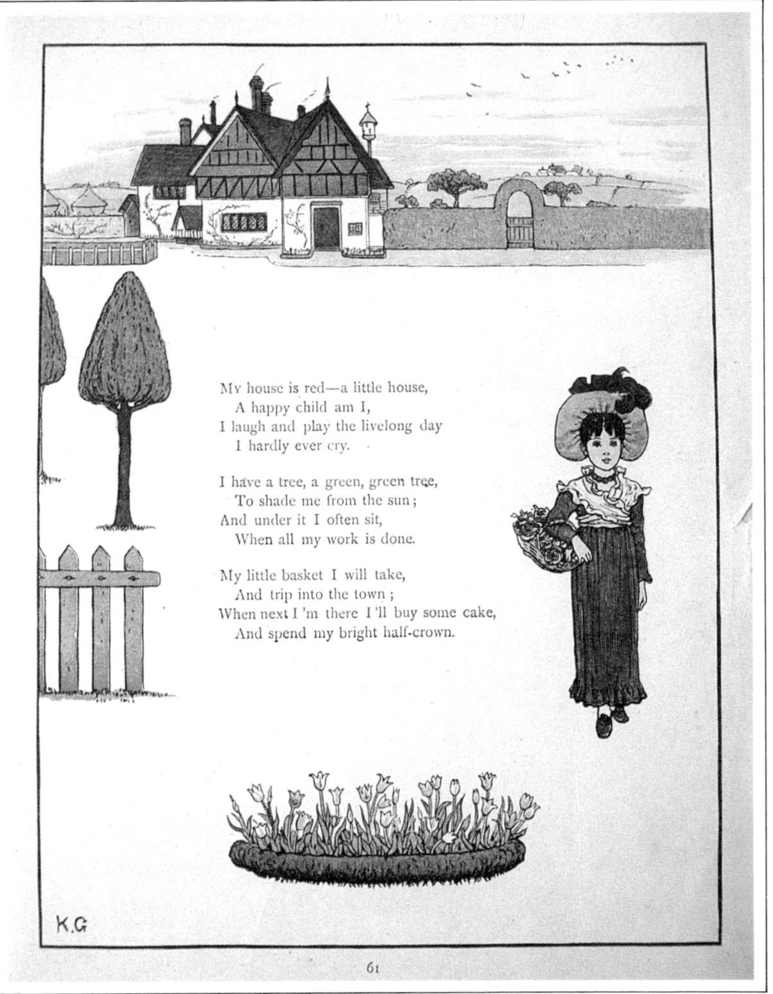

Edmund Evans's home, Leybourne, at Witley in Surrey was the model for this house. The details of the timber-framing, gables and finials are reproduced exactly in this page from UNDER THE WINDOW.

Opposite:
A beautiful study of apple blossom, which was a subject Kate loved to paint; it appears in the background of many pictures.

SING A SONG OF SIXPENCE.

Sing a song of sixpence, a pocket full of rye,
Four-and-twenty blackbirds baked in a pie ;
When the pie was open'd the birds began to sing,
Was not that a dainty dish to set before a King.

Opposite, above:
These picturesque cottages near the church at Witley, Surrey, were also drawn by Birket Foster and Charles Edward Wilson. Kate intended to use them in the background to one of her nursery illustrations.

Opposite, below:
A charming nursery scene which Kate drew for her young friend Lily Evans, daughter of her publisher.

Above:
Nursery rhymes provided Kate with an endless source of inspiration and the excuse to indulge in flamboyant costumes, as in this illustration for 'SING A SONG OF SIXPENCE'.

Above, left:
Frederick Locker-Lampson as seen through the lens of Julia Margaret Cameron.

One of Kate's rare portraits of a man. This one is of her mentor Frederick Locker-Lampson, painted in the early 1880s, and was given to him as a present. It is interesting to compare Kate's impression of him with the photographic portrait by Julia Margaret Cameron (page 53, left).

Right:
Two of the four Locker-Lampson children painted as a gift for their mother in 1883.

One of the most influential people she was introduced to by Evans was Frederick Locker-Lampson, a well-connected dilettante who had published a popular volume of poetry a few years earlier. He was the person Evans approached to look over Kate's verses and make any essential changes before publication. Locker-Lampson, however, took his role of adviser a stage further and, to Kate's intense embarrassment, turned up at the studio she shared with her father in Islington. It was hardly surprising she should have been overawed by this very rich middle-aged gentleman who, Tennyson said, 'looked like a famished and avaricious Jew'.[3] But Locker-Lampson was charming and made it clear he held her work in such high regard that he wanted to help her become better known.

Locker-Lampson was quite sincere in his wish to assist Kate Greenaway's rise to fame. With a plentiful supply of time and money, he liked to cast himself in the role of patron of the arts and had tried to assist struggling artists in the past. These had been men who, whilst being prepared to accept his commissions, were reluctant to let him direct their art and their lives. Kate Greenaway was a totally different proposition. She was flattered by the attentions of this distinguished-looking member of the upper class and more than willing to let him become her mentor.

Within a short time Miss Greenaway was to be seen around town with Mr Locker-Lampson, either discussing the merits of paintings in the National Gallery, or considering Stothard prints for sale in an exclusive shop in the Strand. He escorted her to private viewings of art exhibitions where it was more important to be seen than to see. There she was introduced to aristocrats and luminaries from the worlds of literature and art who had previously only been names to her.

When it was clear he had won her over, Locker-Lampson set about educating Kate to fit more easily into this new society. There were visits to the British Museum for her to learn the finer points of paintings, manuscripts and porcelain. She was also invited to visit his home at Rowfant, Sussex, where his second wife and young

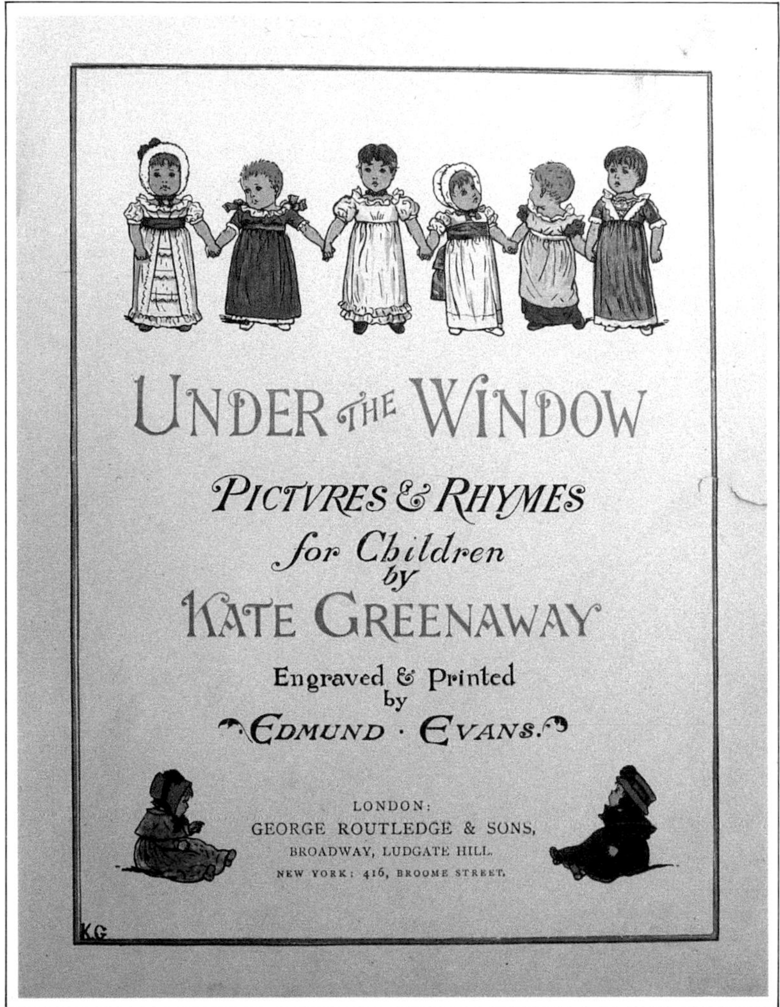

The title page of Kate's first, hugely successful book. Her children were widely copied; the little baby at the end of the line was soon reproduced as a candle snuffer by the Royal Worcester Porcelain Company.

family resided. A potentially difficult meeting passed off easily, for Mrs Locker-Lampson saw that though Miss Greenaway was quite besotted with her husband, she was a safe protégée for him and relieved her of the obligation to be in town.

As Kate learned what to admire and what to shun, she came to the conclusion it would be advantageous for her to move to a more respectable area than the tradesmen's end of Islington. The likely earnings of *Under The Window* rocketed as Edmund Evans told Kate he had persuaded Routledge to produce a phenomenal 20,000 copies for the first printing. Based on this and her earnings from other illustrating work, Kate and her father shared the cost of a lease on a house in Pemberton Gardens, Holloway. This was a higher-class residential area and the house possessed two important features for Kate – space to have a studio at home, and a garden.

This first garden was planted in accordance with her memories of the cottage gardens she had known in Nottinghamshire. Scented roses were a vital ingredient, she believed, and as they flourished in her garden so they did in her art. Carefully painted backgrounds of flowers, drawn in her garden or from the containers which decorated her studio, began to appear in Kate's paintings.

REFERENCES

1 McLean p65
2 Spielmann and Layard p49
3 *My Confidences* F Locker-Lampson p14

4
The Height of Fashion

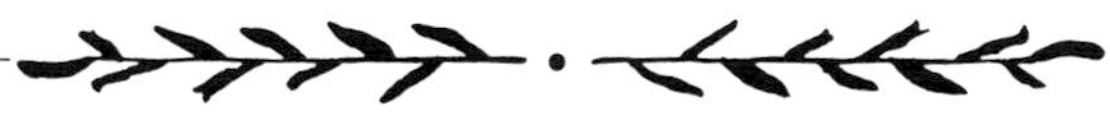

Smocks and sunbonnets are essential garments in the Greenaway pastoral wardrobe.

Under the Window appeared in the shops in October 1879 ready for Christmas. Edmund Evans recalled: 'George Routledge "chaffed" me considerably for printing 20,000 first edition of a book to sell at six shillings, but we soon found out that we had not printed nearly enough to supply the first demand: I know booksellers sold copies at a premium, getting ten shillings each for them: it was, of course, long out of print, for I could not print fast enough to keep up the sale.'[1] With a further 70,000 copies printed and sold in England as well as editions in America and other European countries in subsequent years, Kate Greenaway had achieved instant stardom at the age of thirty-three.

She not only achieved commercial success, but also drew praise from the critics. For the first time she received numerous fan letters. The one which pleased her most was from that doyen of the Victorian art world, John Ruskin. He wrote a long, friendly letter at the beginning of January 1880 complimenting her on her 'gifts' and 'graces' and claiming he had lain awake a quarter of the night thinking of all the things he wanted to tell her. At the same time he mentioned one or two weaknesses in her technique but helpfully suggested ways in which she might remedy them. It was a most unexpected and welcome letter from such an eminent critic.

Almost before the ink had dried on the second edition of *Under The Window*, Edmund Evans was urging Kate to think about her next book, for the 1880 Christmas market. From their discussions emerged the idea for *Kate Greenaway's Birthday Book For Children*, with her name now taking precedence on the cover. They decided on a small format, appropriate to a child's hand and, though there were to be 382 drawings, only twelve would be coloured. This reduced the printing time and ensured the book could be in the bookshops by the autumn. Once the project was arranged, Evans tactfully suggested that Kate concentrate all her energies on the pictures, leaving the 365 verses to be supplied by the popular children's writer Mrs Sale Barker.

Thanks to Locker-Lampson and her new-found fame, Kate's social life took on a different shape in the 1880s. She began

When Kate worked in pen and ink, she always drew with a quill pen. This can be seen on the desk in her portrait on page 95.

receiving invitations to upper-class dining- and drawing-rooms. Prestigious though these invitations were, Kate only accepted a few because she felt ill at ease amongst the cream of smart society: 'a crow amongst beautiful birds' was how she described herself.[2] Nevertheless she happily attended musical evenings, amateur theatricals or the occasional tea-party.

Kate found herself taken up by the leading society hostess, Lady Jeune. The lady's drawing-room was the hub of London society. It was said that if ever a fire broke out and her guests perished, half the peerage would go, royal academicians would be decimated, theatres closed, the pulpits dumb, science would be at a standstill and gaps would appear in the royal family.

Lady Jeune was exceptionally kind to Kate, taking care to invite her only to those functions where she would feel comfortable. As well as taking tea with her ladyship in Wimpole Street, Kate was invited to stay at the family's Berkshire country residence, Arlington Manor. Visits begun in 1880 continued to the end of Kate's life, with her regularly enjoying summer holidays there and joining the large number of house guests over the New Year. Hearing Kate express a longing to meet some member of the royal family, Lady Jeune arranged for her to go to Buckingham Palace in July 1881 and meet the Queen's eldest daughter, Victoria, the Crown Princess of Germany. Such a personal invitation far exceeded Kate's wildest dreams, and through the kind intercession of Lady Jeune other meetings with royalty followed.

The people to whom Locker-Lampson introduced Kate were ideal patrons, and sales and commissions for children's portraits often resulted. Kate was impulsively generous and, far from earning large sums from her paintings, she frequently gave them away to those who had treated her kindly.

The paintings she exhibited at the Royal Academy now attracted much attention and sold easily. As her fame increased so

Above:
Arlington Manor near Newbury, Berkshire, the country house of Sir Francis and Lady Jeune. Kate stayed here frequently, mingling with aristocrats and royalty.

Opposite:
A picture by Miss Greenaway (we scarcely like a bit of it)
Is rightly titled 'Misses' for she hasn't made a hit of it.
So reported the magazine FUN *after this painting was exhibited at the Royal Academy in 1879; but the public disagreed.*

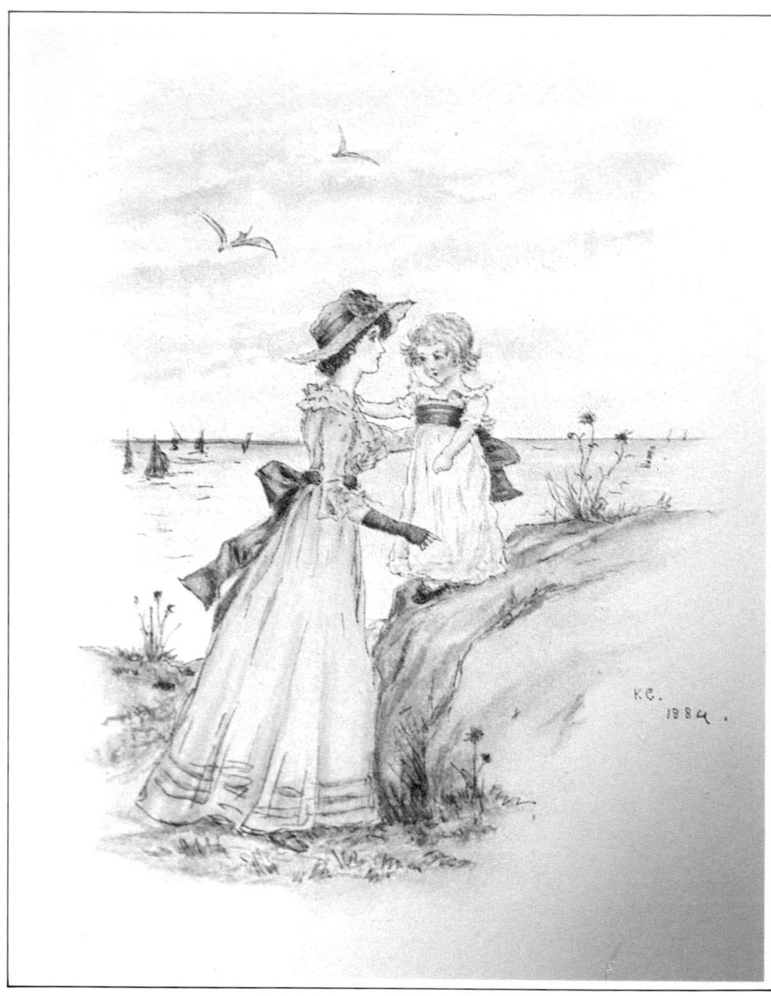

A seaside scene painted at Cromer, Norfolk, during one of Kate's regular summer holidays with the Locker-Lampson family. She presented the painting to John Ruskin in 1884.

Opposite:
Entitled 'A SAILOR'S WIFE', this watercolour was painted at Cromer in Norfolk and reproduced in the Christmas 1894 issue of THE ENGLISH ILLUSTRATED MAGAZINE.

did the adverse comments. One magazine, commenting on her watercolour 'Misses' exhibited in 1879, was quick to make play with the title, writing in pseudo-Greenaway verse:

> A picture by Miss Greenaway (we scarcely like a bit of it)
> Is rightly titled 'Misses', for she hasn't made a hit of it.[3]

Criticism like that might well have upset Kate if Locker-Lampson had not been at hand. He taught her to be realistic about the press, taking notice of valid comments but ignoring the sour grapes. In the case of the 'Misses' painting he pointed out that the painting's ready sale was a clear indication of how misplaced those remarks had been.

Kate Greenaway saw herself in *Punch* at the end of 1880 featured in a Linley Sambourne cartoon entitled 'Christmas is Coming'. Mr Punch is seen reclining in his chair surrounded by a host of figures about to profit from the seasonal festivities. The faces include Marcus Ward peeping through an envelope, Tom Smith dragging a cracker and the three children's book illustrators, Caldecott, Crane and Greenaway. The matronly Miss Greenaway, decked out in bonnet and muff, looked 'a horror', one of her friends declared, but Kate was not too concerned. She was grateful to be thought sufficiently important to parody at all.

Frederick Locker-Lampson undoubtedly had a good influence on Kate. He brought her out of herself and heightened her confidence. Until she met him, Kate had rarely travelled anywhere on her own, but with his encouragement she journeyed by train to Norfolk to stay at his family's seaside retreat at New Haven Court, Cromer, and thereafter she regularly took the train to visit the country houses of various patrons. As Locker-Lampson pointed out, provided she travelled first class, which she could now afford to do, she would be safe.

Intellectually also, Locker-Lampson sought to widen Kate's horizons, urging her to read to make up for the deficiencies in her education. It would boost her confidence in society, he suggested, if

K. Greenaway

she had some subject ready to open a conversation. He continued to oversee Kate's poetic outpourings, correcting her spelling and grammar and trying to shape the whole into a more professional piece of writing.

In matters of business and career too he was a great asset, checking that Evans's offers to Kate matched those made to the male illustrators, Caldecott and Crane. In dealing with Edmund Evans, Locker-Lampson need not have worried about fairness for, as a member of the Society of Friends, Evans was scrupulously fair in all personal and business dealings, never discriminating between men and women.

Locker-Lampson made no monetary gain from his efforts, nor did he seek to: he simply enjoyed the opportunity to manage another's career. Kate was grateful for his advice and interest in her as a person but she did not prove as pliable as he had expected. Evans's observations about her being 'strong-minded' were true. Greenaway and Locker-Lampson did experience differences of opinion and occasionally parted company, only to reunite a few days later. Each needed the other. Kate was in love with this father figure, feeling safe with an older man who was already attached. Locker-Lampson on the other hand was pleased to escape the religious austerity of his young American wife. Fortunately for him, Jane Locker-Lampson was so preoccupied with child bearing and rearing in their country houses that she did not interfere in his London life.

The only adverse effect of Kate's friendship with Locker-Lampson was that she was encouraged to overstretch herself financially. Her friend educated her taste in quality art furnishings. He advised her on collecting old Chelsea porcelain, presented her with some choice pieces and urged her to buy more. His suggestions as to which shops currently stocked good examples and what she should offer for them made Kate feel obliged to purchase.

It also meant that no sooner were the Greenaway family installed at 11 Pemberton Gardens, Holloway, than Kate contemplated having a house designed especially for her. Once again, this was the influence of Locker-Lampson, for Kate and her family had been delighted with the large new house in Holloway with its garden and art studio, far surpassing anywhere they had previously lived. Kate's patron, however, believed she should lead the life of the successful artist, not that of the spinster daughter.

Urged on by him, she spent two thousand pounds, a substantial chunk of her *Under The Window* earnings, on a plot of land at Hampstead. The choice of place was Kate's, though it met with Locker-Lampson's approval since many artists had settled in that area. This did not interest Kate, for it was the association with her childhood which attracted her. Walks across the Highgate fields from Islington to Hampstead had been a regular Sunday morning treat when Kate was a child. Once at the Heath, the little Greenaways had played amongst the flowers, watched by their mother and sketched by their father. In contrast to the backyards and streets of Islington, Hampstead had seemed like the countryside to little Kate, second only in her mind to her beloved Rolleston.

The Greenaway house was to be built on an acre of land facing on to fields in Frognal, which was a country lane on the Finchley side of Hampstead. From what she had heard in society drawing-rooms, Kate understood Richard Norman Shaw to be the most fashionable architect of the day, so he was commissioned to design her house. This was to be one of the smallest properties Shaw designed, for he was frequently engaged to draw plans for large town houses in Kensington, country mansions like Preen Manor and even public buildings like Strangeways Prison. However, he lived in Hampstead himself and had designed other artists' houses in that area, so he was an ideal choice. One thing he prided himself on was suiting the house to the client: hence his design for Miss Greenaway resembled a doll's house.

Her family looked on their newly rich member as provider. Mrs Greenaway, the most business-like member of the family, had relinquished her shop when they moved to Holloway in 1879; Mr Greenaway continued his wood engraving for longer, but as he was nearing seventy decided to retire. Kate's brother Johnny felt himself

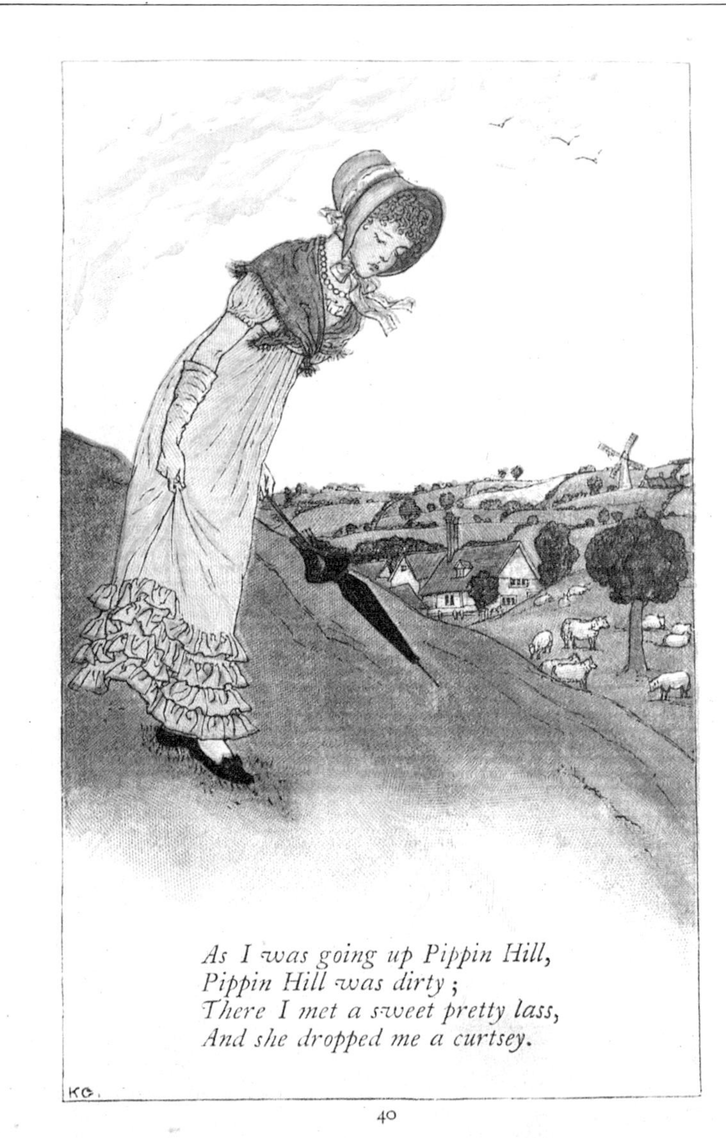
As I was going up Pippin Hill,
Pippin Hill was dirty;
There I met a sweet pretty lass,
And she dropped me a curtsey.
KG.
40

The lass who walks down Pippin Hill in this nursery rhyme is actually passing Tigbourne Farm in Surrey. Kate, in common with her friend Helen Allingham, produced a full-sized watercolour of this delightful old farmhouse near Witley. The windmill in the background is a feature Kate added from her Nottinghamshire memories.

relieved of the obligation to provide for ageing parents and a spinster sister now that Kate was earning vast sums. He decided to indulge his interest in chemistry and took a post at the Royal Chemistry Society as sub-editor of its journal.

It was hardly surprising the family expected Kate to finance them, for her earnings in the early 1880s regularly exceeded a thousand pounds per annum. In addition to the special Kate Greenaway books, she continued to accept commissions to illustrate magazines, books and cards. The public, it seemed, could not buy enough of Kate Greenaway's work. The *Birthday Book*, which appeared in 1880, sold more than 150,000 copies, and earned Kate over eleven hundred pounds. That same year her illustrations appeared in another eighteen books, eight journals and a calendar.

She followed the success of the *Birthday Book* with the publication in September 1881 of a collection of old nursery rhymes which she selected and wrote down from memory herself. *Mother Goose* contained colour illustrations on all forty-eight of its pages. Some criticism was expressed about this book: the version of the nursery rhymes Kate had used was not the proper one; the children looked so miserable; the artist Stacey Marks pointed out that the girl walking down Pippin Hill, in the nursery rhyme of that name, was performing an impossible feat – 'How about the centre of gravity, madam?' he demanded. In a personal letter to Kate he remarked discreetly that she seemed 'so happy and so fearless of all the conventional rules and ideas that obtain about the art' of drawing figures.[4]

Some of the criticisms Kate received should more properly have been directed towards Edmund Evans. The blurred faces, very dark colours and overlapping lines which marred some copies of the book were the fault of the printer. But *Mother Goose* was a book where author and printer had not worked fully in harmony. Against Evans's advice, Kate had insisted the book be printed on a rough-textured paper to resemble old-fashioned hand-made paper. In Evans's opinion this was neither suited to the delicacy of her art nor to his method of wood-block printing. However, since the author remained adamant, Evans invented a method of production whereby the required paper was first flattened between copper plates, then printed and dried, before being dipped in water to restore the rough texture. All of this took extra time and Evans was obliged to speed up the production as much as possible for the book had to reach the shops in time for Christmas 1881. To achieve this, Evans had eliminated the proof-checking stage, denying Kate the opportunity to check the printer's inks against her watercolour originals. When she ultimately saw the finished copy, she was very disappointed.

However, most magazines once again praised her work. After seeing *Mother Goose*, one editor wrote that if children were permitted to elect their favourite goddess 'on a show of tiny hands being taken, the chairman would declare that Miss Greenaway had been unanimously elected for the honour'.[5] Another eminent art journal maintained that if Miss Greenaway had done no more than *Mother Goose* she would yet have done enough. 'Her place among nursery superstitions will be an honourable and good one for many and many a year.' Sales of 66,000 copies in England and Europe demonstrated the public's delight in her book.

Kate had no time to rest on her laurels for Edmund Evans was once again pushing her. For Christmas 1882 he wanted her to try something slightly different. He suggested a collaboration between Kate and his nephew, Myles Birket Foster, son of the famous watercolourist. As the newly appointed organist at the Foundling Hospital, London, Myles Foster planned to produce a book of songs for children. The obvious person to illustrate such a book of words and music was Kate Greenaway. Possibly owing to the family relationship, Evans chose to overlook the fact that music books, even illustrated ones, rarely sold well. Kate was unaware of this. Consequently she was upset to find *A Day in a Child's Life* was not as popular as her previous books. Although this book contained some exquisite flower paintings, only 25,000 copies eventually sold. This never covered the production costs, let alone generated any profit for Kate to receive the agreed half share.

The title page to MOTHER GOOSE, *published in 1881. John Ruskin was captivated by the baby asleep in a basket of roses. The same wicker basket features in many of Kate's pictures in various sizes and guises.*

Opposite:
Her art student training at a branch of the South Kensington School taught Kate an excellent sense of layout and design, as seen here on the title page of her fourth book published in 1882.

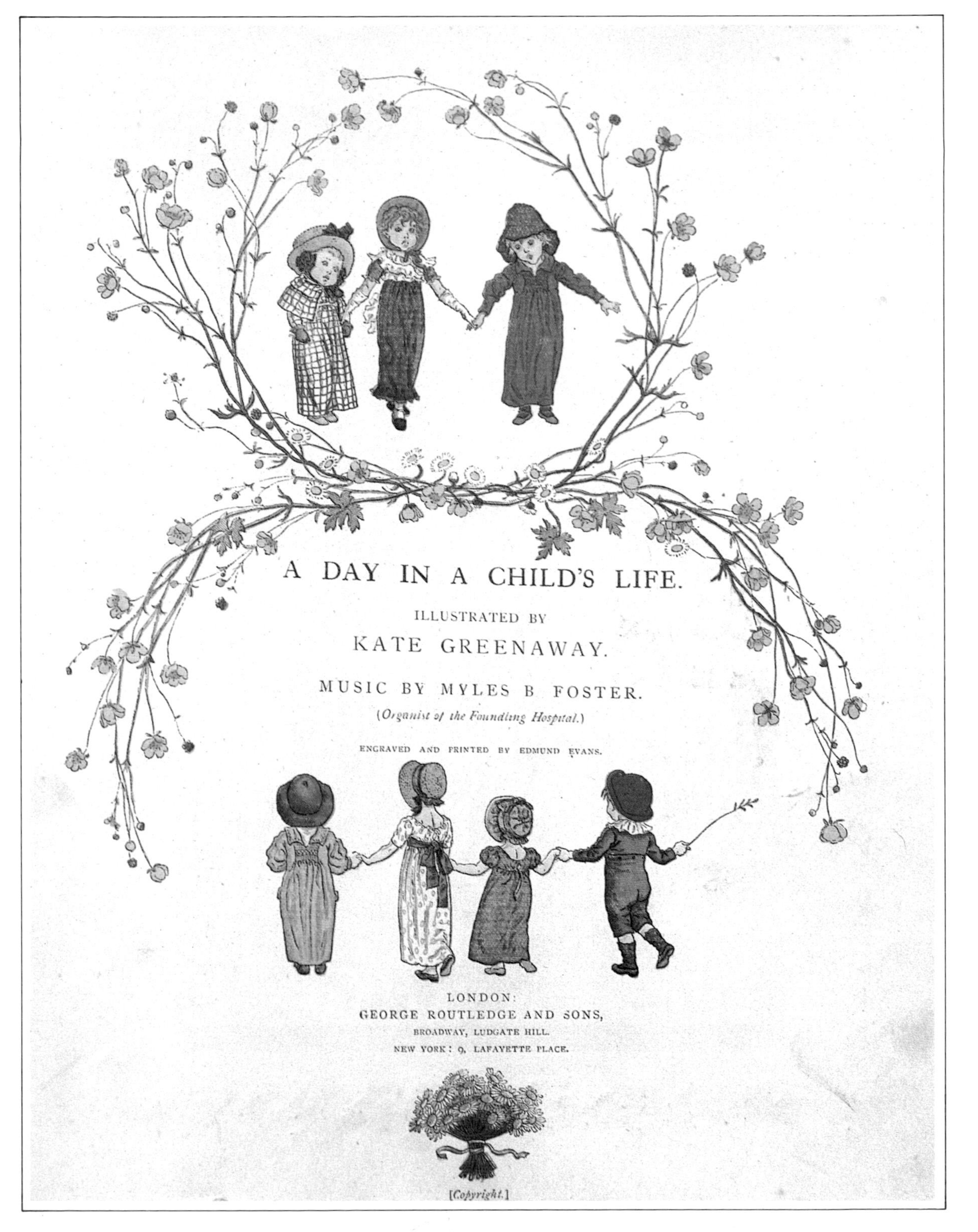

A DAY IN A CHILD'S LIFE.
ILLUSTRATED BY
KATE GREENAWAY.
MUSIC BY MYLES B FOSTER.
(Organist of the Foundling Hospital.)
ENGRAVED AND PRINTED BY EDMUND EVANS.
LONDON:
GEORGE ROUTLEDGE AND SONS,
BROADWAY, LUDGATE HILL.
NEW YORK: 9, LAFAYETTE PLACE.
[Copyright.]

The Locker-Lampson family proved such good friends to Kate that she dedicated her book LITTLE ANN AND OTHER POEMS *to the children and used this portrait of the four of them on the frontispiece.*

The following year Kate returned to a tried and tested formula, that of the illustrated book of verse. She chose a selection from her own childhood favourites, the poets Ann and Jane Taylor, and began drawing pictures to put to fifty of their verses for the book *Little Ann and Other Poems*. At Evans's suggestion she also planned illustrations for an almanac which was to sell at one shilling. This small monthly calendar book with Greenaway drawings filled a niche in the market. Demonstrating his sound business sense, Evans printed a vast number, some with blank space for foreign calendars to be inserted. Thus the 1883 *Almanack* sold 90,000 copies in England, America, France and Germany.

An indication of Kate's enormous popularity was that anything bearing a Greenaway drawing would sell. As a result publishers she had worked for in the past reissued her work. Since they had purchased her early drawings outright, they paid her no royalty but profited handsomely from the fashion she had created. Others commissioned artists to draw 'Greenaway children' and used these pictures either to issue similar nursery books or to decorate porcelain. Devotees of the Aesthetic movement made up dresses for their children to wear from the illustrations in Kate's books. The public, it seemed, could not see enough of the Kate Greenaway style.

REFERENCES

1 McLean p61
2 Letter from Kate Greenaway to John Ruskin 3 April 1898
3 *Fun* magazine 1879
4 Letter from H Stacey Marks to Kate Greenaway 11 Oct 1881
5 Spielmann and Layard p100

CURLY LOCKS.

Curly Locks, Curly Locks, wilt thou be mine ?
Thou shalt not wash dishes nor yet feed the swine,
But sit on a cushion and sew a fine seam,
And feed upon strawberries, sugar, and cream.

'CURLY LOCKS' washes up in the Chappell's Nottinghamshire farmhouse with the familiar grandfather clock and chairs in evidence. The geraniums on the window sill provide unexpectedly rich colour for this illustration.

Opposite, above:
Kate's portrayal of childhood is always a romantic one; it is rare for her to depict a child with any disability. The poem she was illustrating in LITTLE ANN *left her no option.*

Opposite, below:
Kate saw these parrot tulips in a bowl at the home of her publisher Edmund Evans and was so fascinated by their shapes that she sketched them. When she used the design for her book A DAY IN A CHILD'S LIFE *she painted in one of her favourite blue and white bowls.*

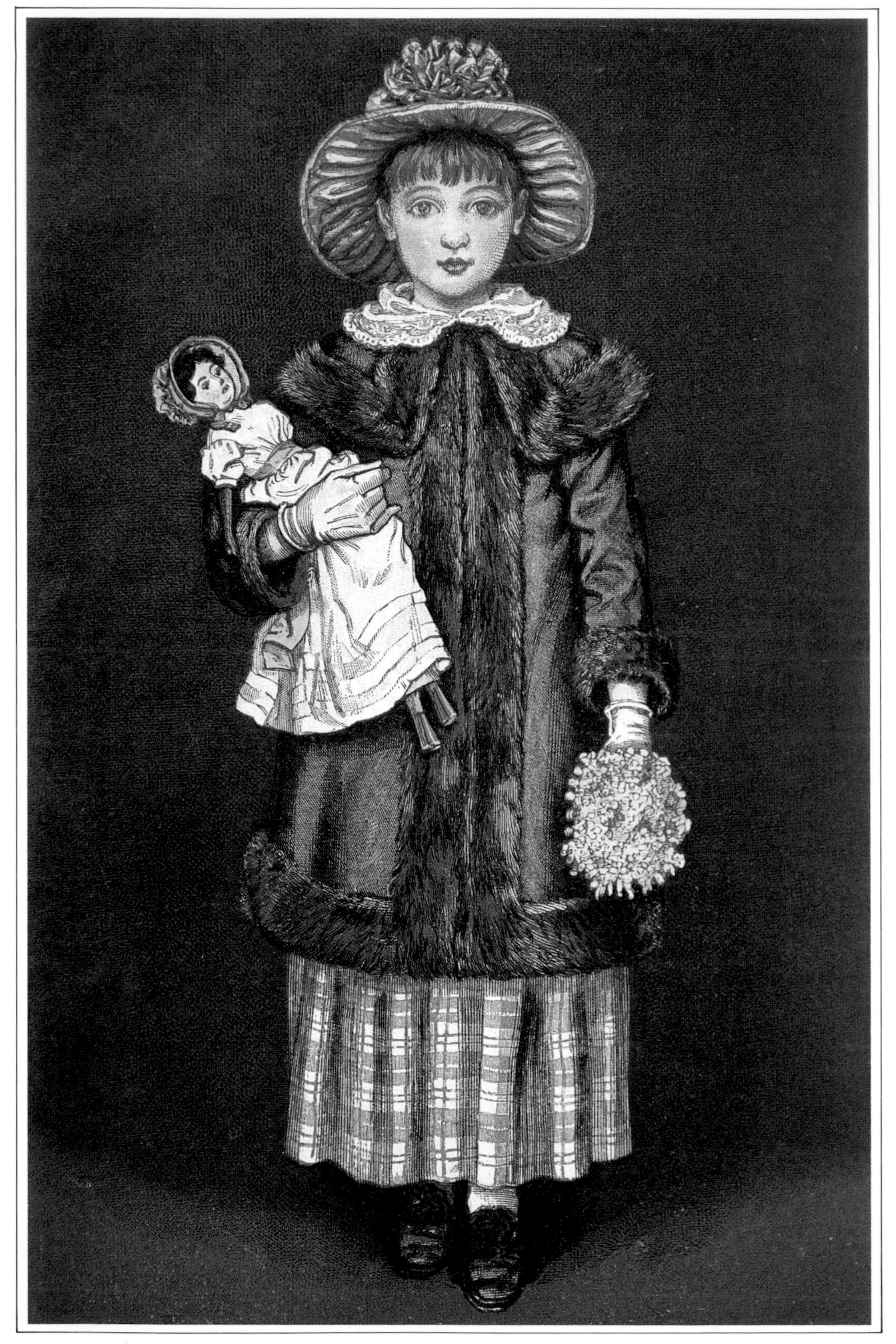

5

The Advent of Professor Ruskin

Opposite:
'Early primrose' formed the frontispiece to the LITTLE WIDE-AWAKE ANNUAL *in 1885. The magazine was intended for children around the age of ten and cost threepence a month.*

ONE OF THE GREATEST COMPLIMENTS Kate ever received about her work was from the art critic John Ruskin who, on seeing one of her drawings of a little girl, wrote immediately to tell the artist that to his mind it was a greater thing than Raphael's St Cecilia. Although Kate received the first communication from the Professor, as she termed him in deference to his position as Slade Professor of Art at Oxford, at the beginning of January 1880, it was almost three years before she actually met the man. In the intervening time they corresponded, at first enthusiastically, but then their letters became spasmodic, interrupted by Mr Ruskin's visits abroad and his silences, during which Kate presumed him to be occupied in greater artistic enterprises. However, as she was to discover later, this was far from the truth.

When Ruskin wrote on Christmas Day 1882 to thank her for the hand-painted Christmas greetings card and copy of her new *Almanack*, he insisted he must bring his thanks in person to Miss Greenaway. Kate was flattered but terrified, being only too aware that this man was revered above all others in the art world. Whatever John Ruskin said or wrote about a painter was widely noted and shaped that artist's reputation. Furthermore, despite her friendship with Frederick Locker-Lampson and her entry into society, Kate remained a shy person. 'Often at first I do not get on with people (especially men)', she was to confide in John Ruskin several years later.[1] Her only comfort was that the Professor was virtually the same age as her father and she felt more at ease with that age group than with younger men.

In the event, their first meeting passed pleasantly. Kate found Mr Ruskin to be a quiet, kindly individual who shared her delight in discussing childhood. In subsequent meetings and letters they were able to reminisce about their own youth and recall favourite stories and rhymes. Far from being critical of Kate's predilection for the nursery world, Ruskin was eager to share in it, confessing he always slept in his old nursery with its comforting bars at the window when he stayed at his London house at Herne Hill. In their conversations Kate and Ruskin occasionally indulged in pretend baby-talk, as Ruskin was so fond of doing with his cousin and companion, Joan Severn.

A small single-sheet Christmas card by Kate Greenaway produced in 1881 by Marcus Ward. Unlike a modern card there was no space for the sender to write their name. On the reverse of the card is printed a verse.

Opposite, above:
Kate's preliminary designs for this title page are detailed and minute.

Opposite, below:
The aged John Ruskin photographed at Brantwood in the 1880s when Kate was a regular visitor.

The letters which Kate now received from Ruskin became ever more affectionate. 'Dear Miss Greenaway' gave way to 'My Dear Kate' and by August 1883 became 'Darlingest Katie', with the letter ending 'Ever your loving J.R.'. Ruskin expressed great eagerness for her to come and see his beloved Brantwood in the Lake District at the earliest opportunity. Accordingly he made elaborate plans for

Kate Greenaway
1883

Given to John Ruskin in June 1886, this picture is called 'A MIDSUMMER FAIRY'. Kate liked the dramatic effect of silhouetting a figure against a full sun or moon and used this device on two or three occasions.

Opposite:
Kate Greenaway at her most sentimental. Readers of the 1883 Christmas issue of THE ILLUSTRATED LONDON NEWS *were captivated by this double page entitled 'TISS ME'.*

her first visit in April 1883, ensuring that she travelled by a certain route to view everything from the best possible angle.

The fortnight Kate spent with her 'darling Dinie' was divine and convinced her that the Professor not only valued her art highly but was in love with her. He might be sixty-four and she thirty-six, but the difference in age was of no consequence with so many common interests. John Ruskin immediately occupied centre stage in Kate's life, pushing Frederick Locker-Lampson into the wings, and Kate confidently expected a proposal of marriage to follow.

To exchange Ruskin for Locker-Lampson as the principal adviser in her life was the most disastrous move Kate ever made. Her luck seemed to change overnight. Ruskin gave out advice on her career which wrecked it, his attempts to improve her drawing ability destroyed her confidence and matters she became involved in, which had no connection with Ruskin, were destined to fail. John Ruskin was a jinx for Kate, though certainly not as a result of conscious malevolence on his part, but rather total naïvety on hers.

Gossip in the London drawing-rooms said that John Ruskin

Oh, what has the old man come for?
Oh, what has the old man come for?
To run away with Billy, I say,
And that's what the old man has come for.

Ah, what will Billy's mamma say?
Ah, what will Billy's papa say?
What a dreadful fright
They'll be in to-night!—
Oh, what will papa and mamma say?

was no longer of sound mind. Stories circulated about the art critic flying into such violent rages that he would smash his hand through a glass window. Other people told of Ruskin's reckless extravagance in ordering quantities of early Bibles and manuscripts from London dealers or impulsively doubling his servants' wages. The long periods of silence, which Kate had noticed when corresponding with Ruskin, were in fact caused by complete mental collapses. On these occasions, his cousin Mrs Severn would take him away to Brantwood where he could recuperate out of public gaze.

In 1878 the art world had followed the Ruskin v Whistler libel case, which Mr Ruskin had lost. The judge's decision to award Mr Whistler just one farthing damages for the art critic's insults set the final seal on a farcical case. Most people were aware that Mr Ruskin had never appeared in court to give evidence because of his mental state.

Locker-Lampson never took kindly to being ousted by anyone but especially a person he no longer respected. What Locker-Lampson knew about John Ruskin he was not prepared to tell a maiden lady, so he contented himself with veiled warnings and a few off-hand remarks, such as he supposed Kate would now christen her new Hampstead house 'The Villa Ruskin'. What really troubled Locker-Lampson, however, was his belief that Ruskin was championing Kate's art for a reason that would never have entered her head. John Ruskin was obsessed by young girls. His marriage had been annulled in 1854 amidst great scandal, but as Kate had only been eight years old at the time, she would have known nothing about it. Since then, rumour told of Mr Ruskin being in love with various 'pets' or 'girlies' as he called them and even attempting to persuade their parents to let him adopt them. The more Locker-Lampson heard about Ruskin from Kate, the more convinced he was that it was Kate's child models who were the attraction and not her.

Given the secrecy that surrounded such subjects, it is likely that Kate was never aware of Ruskin's real interest in her. To her he

Some preliminary drawings and finished artwork for one of Kate's books. She had to make the designs the same size as the finished book, and her books usually involved some exceptionally minute work for both artist and engraver.

Opposite:
Kate's depiction of evil frequently involved goblins. This scene from UNDER THE WINDOW *has a nightmarish quality.*

This fine study of 'SHAMROCKS' at Brantwood was painted by Kate in response to John Ruskin's insistence that she practise painting from life. Kate had a keen eye for colour and could reproduce in watercolour the exact shade she saw in front of her.

Opposite:
Old-fashioned rambling roses fastened to trellising appear in the background of many pictures and were drawn from life.

became a god, whose every bidding must be done and who could only be referred to as 'Him' (with a capital letter) in correspondence with a third party for, as she tried to explain to a friend, there seemed 'to be a "holiness" about his words and ideas'.[2]

The advice Ruskin handed down from on high about Kate's art was in complete contrast to that given her by others. Fearing this, Frederick Locker-Lampson had begged Kate not to change her style rashly. 'Vary it, but do not change it', had been his final plea. The elderly artist Stacey Marks, who had known her from her art school days, recognized her strengths and weaknesses and urged her to stay with book illustrating and not attempt to become a watercolour painter. 'You have a *lay* of your own, and do your best to cultivate it. Think of the large number of people you charm and delight by these designs compared with those who can afford to buy paintings. You have a special gift and it is your duty in every sense to make the most of it.'[3]

From the outset Ruskin stressed to Kate in letters and meetings that she must set her sights on higher art forms than book illustrating, which in his opinion was at the lower end of the spectrum. Kate Greenaway must become a real painter and fulfill the great potential he saw in her. To this end he urged her to look closely at nature and paint out of doors. When she stayed at Brantwood, he took her walking and showed her the beauty of the lake, the mountains and the stone wall's with wild flowers growing out of them, urging her to paint scenes like this rather than her favourite formal gardens. One task he set her was to paint a small clump of shamrock growing behind the house which demanded skill in mixing numerous different shades of green. On another occasion out walking they came upon a rock covered in moss and ivy which Ruskin had set other would-be artists to paint. Difficult though Kate found this, she persevered and produced a very fine study (see page 81).

Ruskin's insistence that she pay more attention to perspective and drawing from life was undoubtedly justified. Unfortunately it paved the way for his next suggestion, that she make nude

Kate found hands and feet particularly difficult to draw and made numerous studies to improve her technique.

drawings of her child models which could be posted to him in order that he might check on her artistic progress. Kate was embarrassed by this request and though she did make numerous studies of arms and especially feet, which she felt she drew badly, she continued drawing the children clad in the frocks she had stitched for them.

Edmund Evans, who had a vested interest in Kate Greenaway remaining a children's book illustrator, pressed her to come and stay more often with his family at Witley in Surrey. There she had the use of his studio to paint in and his carriage to go on drives in the Surrey countryside. Relaxed in the country and happy to be participating in the Evans family life, Kate was persuaded to work on further children's books. *Language of Flowers* was the outcome.

Published in 1884, this perennial Victorian favourite, which assigned special meanings to every flower, was Kate's first real opportunity to demonstrate her outstanding ability to paint flowers. Proudly, she sent Ruskin one of the first copies for Christmas that year and received a torrent of criticism in return. 'You and your publishers are both and all geese', he blustered, but conceded that the public were always stupid enough to pay a shilling for a pennyworth of what they liked. 'Tell me what the publishers "propose" now, that I may sympathise in your indignation – and "propose" something very different', he demanded.[4] Here was a dangerous state of affairs for Kate.

Despite his insistence that Kate become a watercolourist, Ruskin was full of suggestions for joint ventures: a botanical guide for children which would be far superior to *Language of Flowers*; a poetry book with his cousin Joan Severn and a children's story book which he would write and Kate could illustrate. The only idea to come to fruition however was the reissue of an early-nineteenth-century children's book with four new verses by Ruskin accompanied by four new drawings by Greenaway. *Dame Wiggins of Lee and her Seven Wonderful Cats* gave no scope whatever for drawing the children she was so good at; instead Kate was obliged to copy the Mrs Punch figure with her cats and add new episodes in their life. Ruskin also insisted the book appear in black and white so

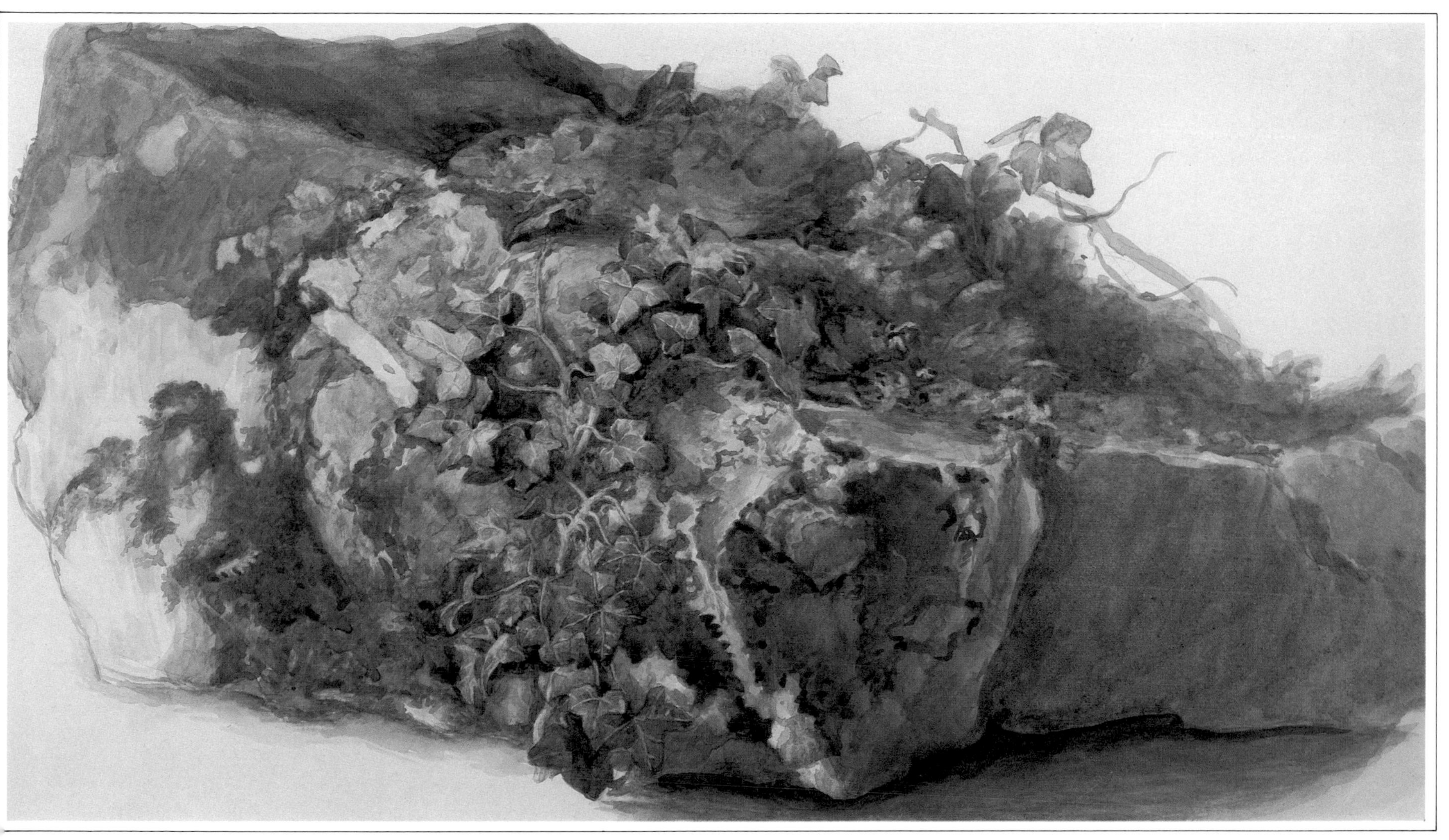

'Study of Rock, Moss and Ivy' was made in 1885 at Ruskin's home, Brantwood, in the Lake District. 'What I remember is that Mr Ruskin proposed to me to do the piece of rock and I said I should like to' Kate recalled. 'Then I remember when I had begun it, he said "Ah, many have begun it" and I remember he wondered at the way I did it.'[5]

'THE FIELD GATE' painted during one of Kate's regular expeditions to Witley, Surrey, where she stayed with the printer Edmund Evans and his family.

that children could colour it in themselves. The resultant drawings are among Kate's worst, but they received lavish praise from the man who mattered most to her.

She was torn between her head, personified by Edmund Evans, and her heart, in the guise of John Ruskin. Listening to Evans, she worked on *Marigold Garden*, the last major book of her own verses and pictures, but she lacked confidence in her abilities. The task took longer than expected and became a grind. The public seemed to sense this, for when it was published in 1885 sales were only 6,500 copies. Ruskin also promptly rubbished it. Kate reported to Joan Severn: 'Mr Ruskin thinks it very bad he says he is ashamed to show it to anyone, I hope it won't affect you so fearfully – I am very very disgusted myself *only I don't feel I'm* so much to blame – as the printers who have literally blotted every picture out.'[6]

Kate grew despondent and confused. Her romance with the Professor was not following a pattern she could understand. At his insistence, Kate paid several visits to Brantwood, where Ruskin encouraged her to enter freely his inner sanctuary. There in his study, he displayed his precious collections of drawings, manuscripts and gemstones, teaching her points to admire in them. At other times he took her on to Lake Coniston. Like a typical suitor with his lady, Ruskin rowed across the water whilst Kate reclined comfortably in the stern of the 'Jumping Jenny'. Not all thought he looked the part of the suitor; a visiting American reported that Mr Ruskin looked 'an old man, with a look even older than his years, with bent form, with the beard of a patriarch, with an habitual expression of weariness, with the general air and gait of age'.[7]

Kate saw only a gentle, loving person who liked to share in her world of make-believe. In the evenings they talked of favourite baby games and stories, taking the parts of some of the characters

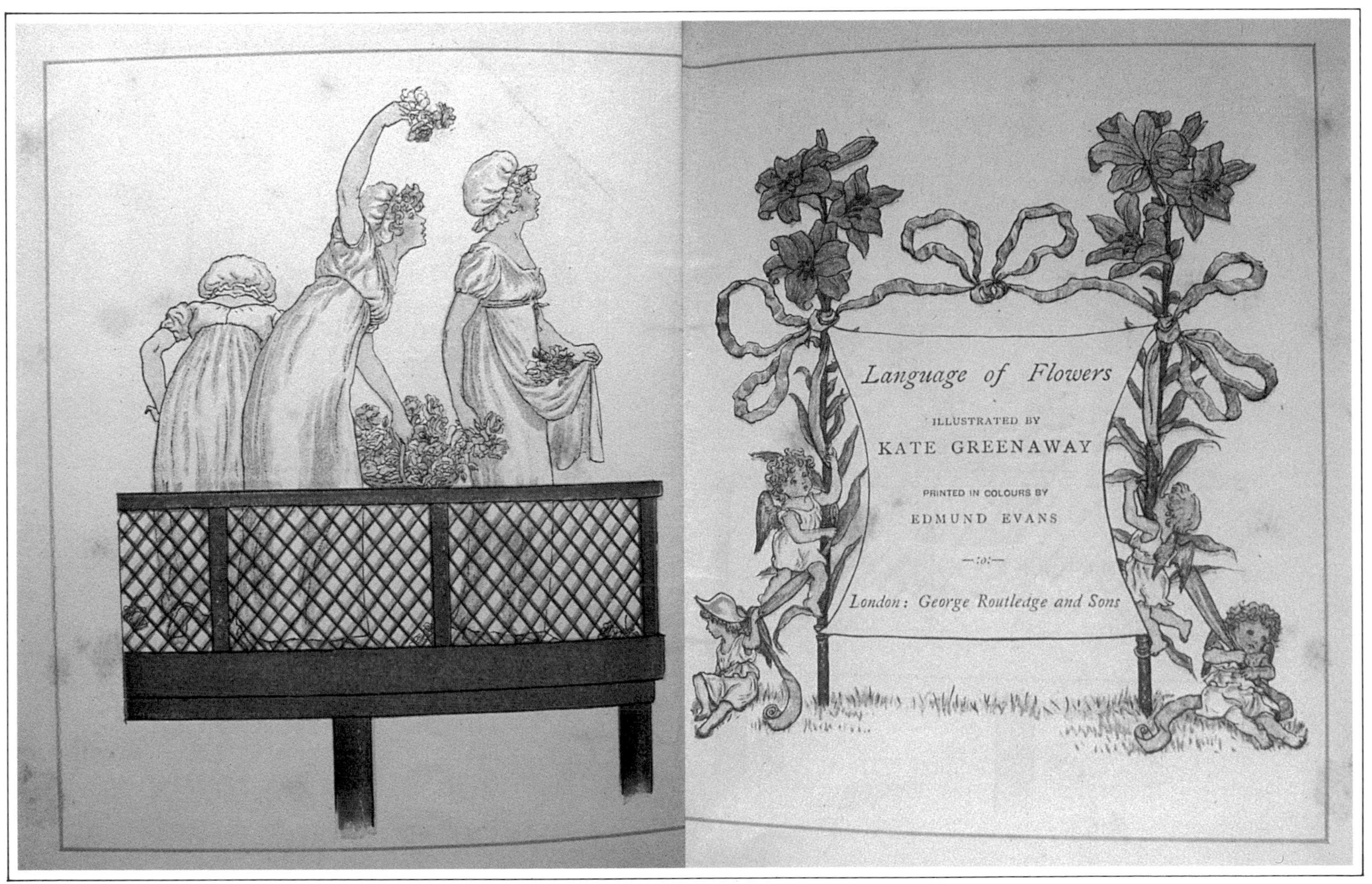

The frontispiece from LANGUAGE OF FLOWERS *in which Kate once more makes use of her favourite trellising, not to support roses this time, but as the sides to a balcony.*

The title page from LANGUAGE OF FLOWERS *published in 1884, which established Kate's fame as a flower painter.*

Narcissus	*Egotism.*
Nasturtium	*Patriotism.*
Nettle, Burning	*Slander.*
Nettle Tree	*Concert.*
Night-blooming Cereus	*Transient beauty.*
Night Convolvulus	*Night.*
Nightshade	*Truth.*

30

A page from LANGUAGE OF FLOWERS *where Kate makes use of the carnation study seen on page 98 (left).*

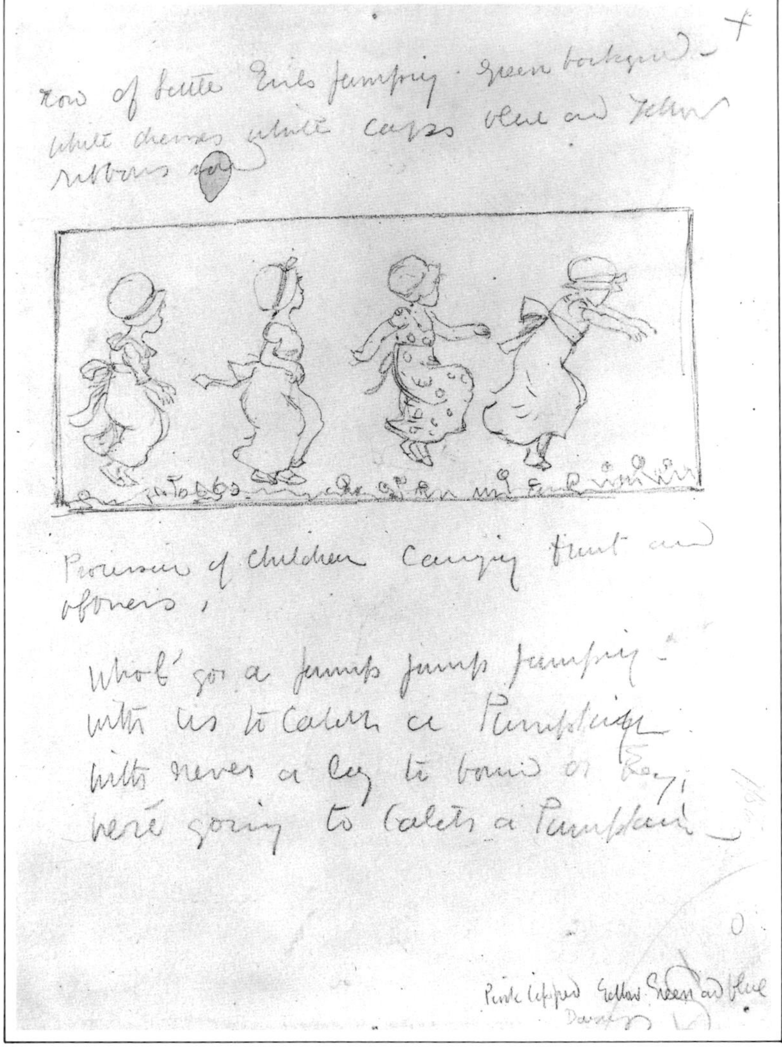

Some preliminary pencilled ideas for the layout of a page in her book MARIGOLD GARDEN, *published in 1885.*

Opposite:
*'*STREET SHOW*' is a watercolour Kate painted for* MARIGOLD GARDEN. *Inspiration for this scene came from the bank holiday crowds she observed on Hampstead Heath.*

KG Kate Greenaway

and creating new episodes. Unfortunately life at Brantwood was not always so peaceful. During Kate's visit in the summer of 1885, Ruskin became so agitated that Joan Severn, recognizing the onset of another mental breakdown, implored Kate to return home. She refused because her beloved Professor begged her to stay with him; she was the only person who really understood and cared for him, he claimed. When the collapse came, Kate was shocked and reluctantly agreed to return home.

In the spring of 1888, when Kate arrived for what was becoming her annual visit, she witnessed one of his most distressing and violent attacks. Although trained attendants had to be fetched to restrain Ruskin, Kate refused to leave, insisting that he needed her. Serious differences of opinion emerged between Kate and Joan Severn, who had the unenviable responsibility for her cousin's welfare. A letter from Mrs Severn to a friend gives an insight into the sad state of affairs: 'Of course the poor Coz was both cruel and foolish in having K.G. on a visit but I believe she pestered him into it and is herself so foolish in the matter – and quite asserts she has a right to expect all sorts of favours from him for the way he has gone on with her – and perhaps she is right, but oh the sorrow, and perplexity of it all – he has got worse and worse.'[8]

Joan Severn knew that Kate Greenaway was only one of several younger women to whom her cousin had written extraordinarily affectionate letters. In most cases he had lauded their art, taken them out on walks to draw the moss-covered rock and persuaded them his love for them was unique. To each he said she was the only person in the world who could understand and help him. Most of the young women were but adolescents and either tired of the Ruskin romance or were warned off by older relatives. Sadly, Kate, moving into unmarried middle age, shut out any contradictory information and clung to her belief in their relationship.

REFERENCES

1 Letter from Kate Greenaway to John Ruskin 28 Oct 1896
2 Letter from F Locker-Lampson to Kate Greenaway 1881
3 Letter from H Stacey Marks to Kate Greenaway 22 Oct 1897
4 Letter from John Ruskin to Kate Greenaway 19 Jan 1885
5 Letter from Kate Greenaway to Joan Severn 2 Feb 1893
6 Letter from Kate Greenaway to Joan Severn 9 Nov 1894
7 Birkenhead p297
8 Letter from Joan Severn to Lady Simon 18 March 1888

Opposite:
Kate was so fascinated by the tile-hung cottages she saw in Surrey that Richard Norman Shaw incorporated the same feature into the house he designed for her in London.

Below:
The mother and baby pose in front of a typical Greenaway piece of topiary in this beautifully designed scene.

THE
GIRL'S OWN
ANNUAL
KG
ILLUSTRATED
LONDON: 56, PATERNOSTER ROW.

6

THE FINAL YEARS

Opposite:
Since many girls had been brought up with Kate's nursery books, Routledge commissioned her to provide illustrations for several of their annuals towards the end of the century. This picture appeared in 1887.

As time went on Kate undertook less work as an illustrator, producing only a further two major works, the *Pied Piper of Hamelin* and *Kate Greenaway's Book of Games.*

It was three years after *Marigold Garden* that she wrote to the poet Robert Browning seeking permission to publish her drawings to his narrative poem which had been one of her own childhood favourites. This granted, she set about researching medieval costume. The finished book, engraved by Evans and published by Routledge, appeared in the autumn of 1888, selling 10,000 copies in England. Reactions were mixed. Those prestigious art magazines who had once been loud in their praise of Greenaway books dismissed the *Pied Piper* as 'pseudo-German medievalism on a large scale' and said the children looked stupid and dull. In America, where Greenaway was still greatly in demand, reviewers were ecstatic, claiming Miss Greenaway had now gained more followers than the Pied Piper himself.

The book also found some favour with John Ruskin who admired Kate's depiction of rats and thought the Piper looked 'sublime'. Ruskin could not, however, resist reminding Kate that she would have done better to have drawn from life and he remarked that the scene where the Piper and children danced in Paradise was a disappointment: 'a *real* view of Hampstead pond in spring would have been more celestial to me than this customary flat of yours with the trees stuck into it at regular distances'.[1] The following year he had forgotten his criticism and referred to the *Pied Piper* as the best book she had ever done.

In 1889 *Kate Greenaway's Book of Games* appeared, with twenty-four colour pages illustrating her own versions of favourite nursery pastimes. The book was a return to the familiar theme of Greenaway children desporting themselves in formal gardens, drawing-rooms and flowery fields, but it struggled to sell the 10,000 copies Evans printed. Kate was further convinced of the wisdom of Ruskin's advice.

During the 1890s her commercial illustrations trickled on with some very fine pictures for Routledge's girls' magazines. The

This interior scene is from Kate's illustrations for the PIED PIPER OF HAMELIN, *which proved immensely popular in America when it was published.*

Opposite, above:
The two children looking at 'rats in other men's hats' are from the PIED PIPER OF HAMELIN. *This had been one of Kate's favourite poems as a child and she approached Robert Browning in 1888 for permission to publish the work with her own illustrations.*

Opposite, below:
Men feature rarely in Greenaway illustrations. Kate borrowed ideas from early Rossetti paintings, which she greatly admired, in order to portray the Pied Piper.

PUSS IN THE CORNER.

THE child who represents puss stands in the middle, while the others stand at fixed stations round her. One then beckons to another saying: "Puss, puss, give me a drop of water!" when each runs and change places. Puss then runs and tries to get into one of the places, if she succeeds, the one left out is puss.

BATTLEDORE & SHUTTLECOCK.

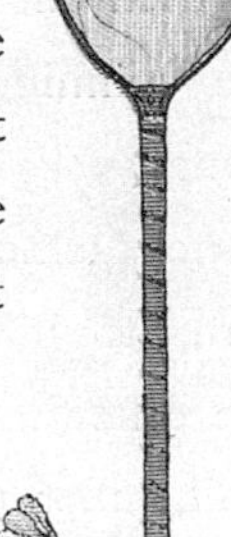

THIS is a most convenient game, because one solitary individual can find amusement as well as any number, provided there is a bat for each player. The object of the game is to keep the shuttlecock going as long as possible.

HOOPS.

EVERY child knows, or ought to know, the pleasure of bowling a hoop. What a nice ring there is about it, when on a fine frosty day the juvenile members of the family all turn out with hoops and race along the road. There is a very jolly game called "turnpikes," but it wants rather an open space; any number can play, only half the

This sketch of children playing was drawn for one of Kate's favourite's, Lily Evans, who lived in Surrey. Lily allowed it to be published in THE GIRL'S OWN PAPER *to accompany the article she wrote celebrating her friendship with the late Miss Greenaway.*

Left, and opposite:
These three colour illustrations are from KATE GREENAWAY'S BOOK OF GAMES *which was published in 1889. The book gave precise instructions on how to play many of Kate's own favourite childhood games.*

K.Greenaway

Almanack, successfully started in 1883, appeared annually until 1895 but Kate regarded this tiny book as little more than hack work and soon ceased to draw new pictures, preferring to recycle ones from her previous publications; nonetheless she was grateful for the income it generated. Ruskin told her that she was merely selling dregs to the public.

Kate's attention turned to producing larger-scale watercolours. She was pleased to receive some recognition for her painting from the Royal Institute of Painters in Watercolour, who elected her a member in 1899. But she was well aware this body was not regarded as highly as the Royal Watercolour Society who had made her former art school friend, Helen Allingham, its first woman member as early as 1875. Helen Allingham's paintings of Surrey cottages were proving immensely popular. Kate had attended Helen's several one-woman exhibitions at the Fine Art Society's galleries in New Bond Street and knew that she sold most of her eighty paintings there each time. Since cottages seemed to be the magic ingredient, Kate decided to alter her subjects.

The friendship between Kate and Helen was strong in 1889 following the Allinghams' move to Hampstead. Mrs Allingham gratefully accepted the offer of joint painting expeditions with Kate in the months following the death of her husband. It was Helen's suggestion that the two women visit Freshwater on the Isle of Wight, where Helen wanted to show her friend the beautiful thatched cottages on Lord Tennyson's estate.

Through Mrs Allingham's friendship with the Poet Laureate, both women received invitations to take tea with him and his family. This led on to a particular friendship between Kate and Lady Tennyson as a result of which Kate became an annual visitor either at the Tennyson's island home or their house in Surrey. In gratitude, she painted portraits of the Tennyson grandchildren as gifts for the family.

Following the Freshwater excursion, Helen proposed painting in Pinner, which was closer to home and easily accessible from Hampstead by rail. In June 1890, Kate and Helen were to be found

An official studio portrait of Kate Greenaway taken when she was in her late forties by the celebrated photographers Elliot & Fry. On the desk is the quill pen which Kate liked to use for pen and ink drawings.

Opposite:

This cottage at Pinner was painted in June 1890 under the guidance of Kate's friend Helen Allingham.

Above:
One of Helen Allingham's paintings of the cottage at Pinner. It is interesting to compare her interpretation with those of Kate Greenaway opposite and on page 94.

Opposite:
The same cottage as on page 94 from a different angle. Kate Greenaway and Helen Allingham were obliged to work quickly as the cottage was scheduled for demolition later the same week.

sitting side by side painting a picturesque cottage scheduled for demolition. They both produced two paintings of the cottage, one front on and the other from the side. Fortunately all four watercolours have survived and it is interesting to compare the artists' treatment of the subject. Helen Allingham added her familiar sun-bonneted mother, child on her arm, standing at the cottage gate, whereas Kate painted a floral foreground with Greenaway children gathering posies of cowslips.

Neither artist felt at ease working alongside the other and tactfully they agreed to part after the Pinner experiment. Kate found the pace of Helen's work, dawn till dusk six days a week, gruelling. Although Kate liked to do her preliminary sketching out of doors, she preferred to paint in morning light in the controlled conditions of her studio. Problems also arose over Kate's short-sightedness: 'What am I to do?' she asked Helen. 'When I look at the roof it is all a red blur – when I put on my spectacles I see every crack in the tiles.'*2*

Kate continued with cottage subjects a little longer but, not surprisingly, found the public comparing her cottage paintings unfavourably with Mrs Allingham's. Dilapidated country cottages with their rampant gardens could never be the right subject for one so neat and orderly as Kate Greenaway. She was happier and more successful depicting beautifully clad children as the central figures against a background of flowers.

Above, centre:
A beautiful pencil sketch of one of Kate's young models.

Above, left:
Studies of some pinks in a flowerpot on the balcony outside Kate's studio at Hampstead, later worked into LANGUAGE OF FLOWERS *(see page 84, left).*

Above, right:
The watercolour study of 'BOY IN A BLUE SMOCK' was probably made from her nephew Eddie Dadd, her favourite boy model.

Kate always cherished the hope that she would become more renowned as a watercolourist than a book illustrator. To this end she consciously imitated the style of the successful cottage artist Helen Allingham.

Back in her studio with her child models, Kate worked every morning, from eight till one. Drawing babies and young children was difficult because they rarely kept still. Any attempt to persuade a child into a pose against its will usually ended in tears and this so contorted the face that drawing was useless. By bribing the infant with biscuits or using an older sister to distract it, Kate contrived to make her sketches. She tried to arrange most of her sketching to take place in the winter when she found the light hopeless for painting. The winter was also a time when she felt at her most imaginative because, as she said, in the midst of snow a cowslip seems a really divine thing.

Afternoons were strictly set aside for relaxation. Kate either walked on Hampstead Heath where she observed the children playing or went into town to gaze in the windows of the brightly lit shops. Window shopping was a favourite pastime of hers, especially in Regent Street. She would spend a long time looking at the fabrics and dresses in Liberty's or watching the pavement artists and street entertainers.

By three o'clock Kate would be ready to return home for afternoon tea, which was the highlight of her day. Re-creating the principal social events in her Rolleston childhood, she liked to invite friends to partake of this meal with her. Kate also found it was convenient to reciprocate the hospitality of her grand friends by inviting them to visit her studio, then take tea in the room adjacent. The incorporation of this special tea-room had been one of Kate's particular requests to Richard Norman Shaw when he was designing the house.

'Watched them go off with their Skates'

Above, right:
Kate photographed in her studio at Hampstead in 1898. In the foreground is one of the rush-bottomed chairs which appear so regularly in her pictures. The podium on which she positioned her child models can also be seen and to the right of it 'Belinda', the lay figure dressed in one of the frocks and bonnets Kate stitched. The door leads through to the tea-room where Kate entertained her friends and patrons.

Right:
Kate usually objected to painting winter scenes because she said the cold made children's complexions go a 'horrid bluey-red'.

In the summer tea was taken out of doors in Kate's beautiful garden. Although she had little experience of gardening, once given the opportunity Kate displayed a talent. Her garden at Frognal was immaculate, with the same gravel paths, neat lawns, formal flower beds and trellised roses as those which appear in her paintings. She cultivated specific plants for her pictures: 'Cinderella', for example, required a row of scarlet-flowering runner beans in the background, she thought. These were duly planted for painting the following summer. Thirty-three lilies were specially grown for the background of her 'Child in a White Dress'. Nature was not always kind to Kate: on one occasion the birds stripped all the cherries off a tree she had begun painting for the background of one picture. Resourcefully she set about tying artifical ones in their place so she could continue with her work.

Kate's evenings were times for needlework. Not only did she stitch the costumes required for her models but she also worked up her own embroidery designs and made soft furnishings for her house. From Kate's correspondence it is possible to glimpse Greenaway interior design. Light apple green featured largely, with wallpaper and blinds being of a similar hue. In her tea-room Kate allowed her imagination full rein and took the theme of a parrot. The walls were papered in deep greeny-blue, the curtains were of apple green, two of the cushions yellow velvet and one rose red – 'the colour you see in the ring round a parrot's neck' she said – whilst the colour of the carpet stool resembled a 'real green parrot'.[3] Kate clearly inherited her mother's excellent eye for colour and design, along with the practical skill to turn them into reality.

In February 1891 Kate held her first exhibition at the Fine Art Society, showing 151 pictures. Originally she had intended to exhibit her new watercolours but these were not ready in time, so she went round the studio collecting up original book illustrations. Only six of the new pictures appeared and the public showed little

These studies for lilies from Kate's sketchbook show that she sometimes began work by making an outline with a loaded paintbrush rather than pencil or charcoal.

Entitled 'PRISSY', this picture was reproduced in LITTLE WIDE-AWAKE: AN ILLUSTRATED MAGAZINE FOR CHILDREN. *Kate's father, John Greenaway, who died in 1890, was often employed to engrave blocks for this magazine.*

A preliminary study of poppies made from a gift sent to Kate by Lady Mayo in Ireland, the daughter of one of Kate's patrons.

Opposite:
The background for this painting 'LITTLE GIRL IN A WHITE DRESS' was Kate's own garden in Hampstead where she grew thirty lilies especially for the picture.

K.G

interest in them. However, sales from the exhibition earned Kate 964 pounds, a useful sum for pictures which had already been paid for once by Edmund Evans.

There were two further exhibitions at the Fine Art Society galleries, one in 1894, the other in 1898, but these were less successful. Whilst members of the public were prepared to purchase some of the pictures they recognized from books, they were reluctant to buy Greenaway watercolours of cottages and landscapes. 'I feel far more that my drawing is not the drawing that is liked just now,' she wrote sadly, 'and also that I am getting to be a thing of the past.'[4]

The 1890s were depressing years for Kate Greenaway. They opened badly with the sudden death of her father in August 1890. She had been closer to him than anyone and felt the loss deeply. Four years later her mother died and Kate no longer had the security of being the child of the family. Throughout all this time she suffered perpetual worries about money. The Hampstead house had cost a fortune to build and furnish, apart from the additional expense of having the garden laid out and planted. Since the whole enterprise had been undertaken by Kate she paid the bills but, because the sums involved were large, payments had been spread over several years. She was still obliged to repay substantial amounts at a time when her income was shrinking. The house proved costly to run, which meant Kate had to undertake some of the housekeeping herself in an effort to economize; this ate into painting time.

Kate searched desperately for other methods of generating income. Although she disliked the restrictions of painting to order, she let it be known she was prepared to undertake portrait commissions of children. Through the kind auspices of Lady Jeune, a few society mothers brought their offspring to be immortalized by Miss Greenaway.

As sales of her watercolours slumped and dealers tried to beat the price down even further, Kate turned to oil painting. Her struggles to master the new medium make sad reading. After a lifetime of using a fine point brush, she said to work with a broad brush was like trying to draw with a pencil without a point. The oil paints themselves caused her problems. At first the paint ran everywhere, then she found it dried too quickly if she worked out of doors. There were problems getting the colours she wanted, for she found when the paint was dry the shade had changed. Eventually she conquered the problems of technique sufficiently to

These three little girls from THE APRIL BABY'S BOOK OF TUNES, *published in 1900, look like Lewis Carroll's Alice.*

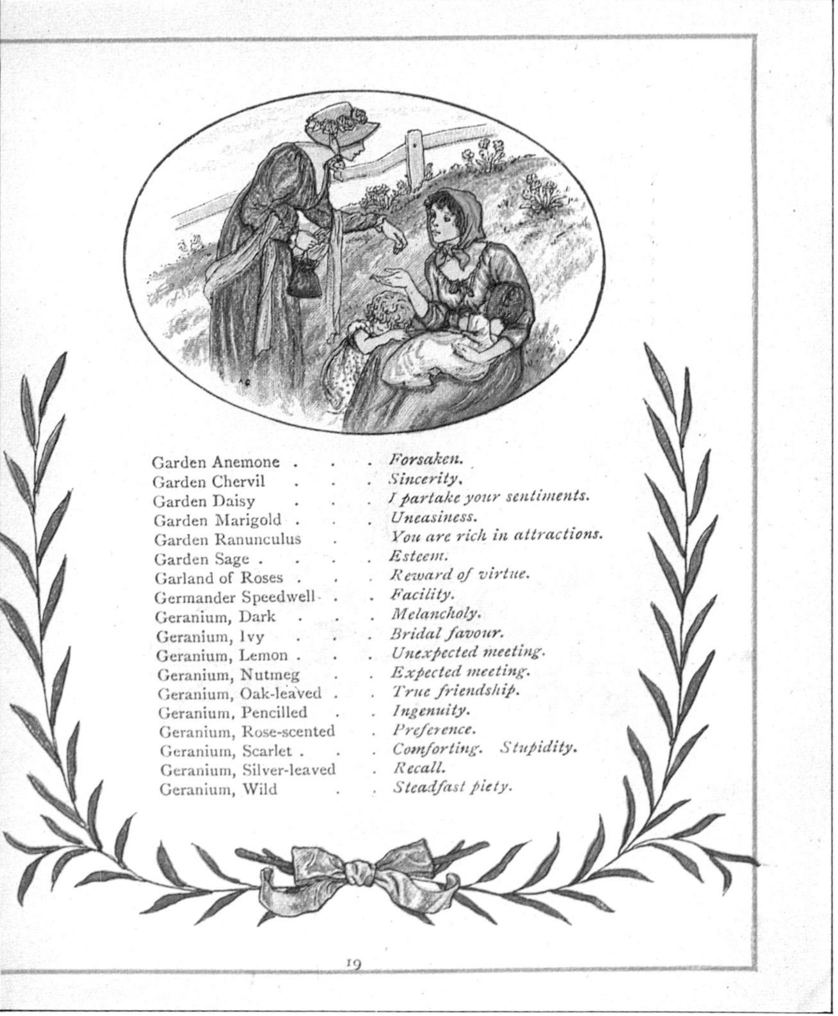

Garden Anemone	*Forsaken.*
Garden Chervil	*Sincerity.*
Garden Daisy	*I partake your sentiments.*
Garden Marigold	*Uneasiness.*
Garden Ranunculus	*You are rich in attractions.*
Garden Sage	*Esteem.*
Garland of Roses	*Reward of virtue.*
Germander Speedwell	*Facility.*
Geranium, Dark	*Melancholy.*
Geranium, Ivy	*Bridal favour.*
Geranium, Lemon	*Unexpected meeting.*
Geranium, Nutmeg	*Expected meeting.*
Geranium, Oak-leaved	*True friendship.*
Geranium, Pencilled	*Ingenuity.*
Geranium, Rose-scented	*Preference.*
Geranium, Scarlet	*Comforting. Stupidity.*
Geranium, Silver-leaved	*Recall.*
Geranium, Wild	*Steadfast piety.*

19

From LANGUAGE OF FLOWERS *is taken this highly romantic portrayal of poverty. Kate herself was to experience financial worries towards the end of her life.*

Opposite:
This version of the nursery rhyme, 'WHERE ARE YOU GOING TO, MY PRETTY MAID?' from THE APRIL BABY'S BOOK OF TUNES, *is interesting to compare with the one on page 24 (left).*

No. 9.
SLEEPING.
1. Lul-la-by, lul-la-by, ba - by dear, Take thy rest with - out a fear;
2. Lul-la-by, lul-la-by, gone is the light, Yet let not darkness my ba - by fright,
3. pp May thy small dreams no ill things see, Kind heaven keep watch, my babe, o'er thee,
Qui - et sleep; for mo-ther is here,..... E - ver wake - ful, e - - ver near,
Mo - ther is with her a - mid the night;.... Then soft - ly sleep, my heart's de - light,
Kind an - gels bright thy guard - ians be,........ And give thee, smil-ing, to day and to me,

Opposite:
Mother and child were a favourite subject of Kate's and dealt with tenderly, as in this picture called 'SLEEPING'.

produce some children's portraits but they bear no comparison with her delicate watercolour work.

Kate was prepared to try anything. At one point she talked to her younger sister Fanny, then married and living close by, about the possibility of setting up a dressmaking business together, but the idea came to nothing. On another occasion she said she would try modelling gesso panels of processions of Greenaway children to sell. Spurred on by the sales of Ruskin's autobiography *Praeterita*, Kate began pencilling down episodes from her own life with a view to writing a book. It never progressed far, though it gave her great pleasure to relive childhood incidents. The fragile exercise book which survives provides a useful window into Kate's early life. She took up poetry, verses concerned with unrequited love, but the four volumes produced were probably too personal for publication. She even began playwriting, but it was all to no avail.

By the time she reached her fiftieth birthday in March 1896, Kate's health was causing concern. She sought the advice of Dr Elizabeth Garrett Anderson and followed up her recommendation to 'learn the bicycle' as a method of combating her indisposition, but the tiredness and depression continued.

The death of John Ruskin in January 1900 upset Kate greatly even though visits and letters from him had ceased several years previously. Since then she had continued writing every few days, hoping her letters might bring him some comfort. She had come to accept the fact that marriage to him was out of the question, but she still cherished the belief that he cared more for her than anyone else.

At the time of Ruskin's death, Kate knew herself to be suffering from breast cancer though she told no one. When she finally agreed to surgery, the condition had deteriorated too far. Kate put on a brave face, insisting that she was simply suffering from rheumatism and colds, but on 6 November 1901 she died at her home in Frognal.

REFERENCES

1 Letter from John Ruskin to Kate Greenaway 23 Feb 1888
2 Spielmann and Layard p173
3 Letter from Kate Greenaway to John Ruskin 11 February 1896
4 Letter from Kate Greenaway to Violet Dickinson 13 March 1898

Dear Willy would a-wooing go.
Hadley
Where are you going to, my pretty maid?
"I'm going a-milking Sir" she said.
Hadley

7

Kate Greenaway for Collectors

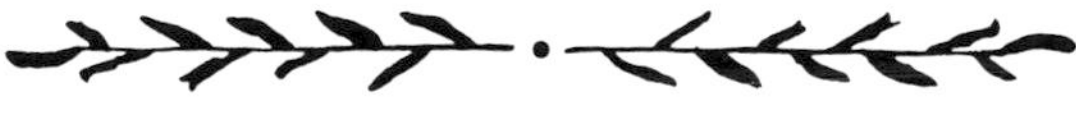

Opposite:

These two terracotta plaques made for framing were modelled by James Hadley of Worcester in the 1890s. Although he made no reference to the source of his inspiration, a comparison with Kate's illustration on page 24 (left) makes it clear.

THE GULF BETWEEN Kate Greenaway the person and Kate Greenaway the style widened towards the end of the nineteenth century. As the one became more retiring, the other detached itself and took on an independent existence. So separate did the two become that many people at the time had no idea the woman existed and a hundred years later Kate Greenaway is thought by some to be simply a brand name.

A few weeks after Kate's death, John Greenaway arranged a fourth exhibition of his sister's work at the Fine Art Society as part of the studio clearance prior to his sale of the Hampstead house. The event was poorly attended and realized little money for the estate, since the show contained mainly pictures that Kate had been unable to sell or finish. The main talking point was a special display case in the centre of the room which contained some illustrated letters Kate had sent to Ruskin. These left plenty of scope for the imagination because, at the insistence of Ruskin's executors, any passages considered 'too intimate and particular' were masked from 'the vulgar eye' by little pieces of paper. The whole event was a sad obituary for a once successful artist.

'It is so difficult now I am no longer at all the fashion – I say fashion, for that is the right word, that is all it is to a great many people,' Kate had written despondently a few years before her death.[1] Her judgement was not entirely correct. The artistic élite, who had taken her up with such alacrity in the early 1880s, had indeed turned their attention to the artists of the Art Nouveau style, but that did not mean the vogue for Kate Greenaway was over. It moved instead from a narrow clique to a wider audience, and by the turn of the century was reaching more people than ever before. Since Kate went about little, and only to the country houses of her former patrons, she remained in ignorance of her new fame.

The publisher Frederick Warne assisted in popularizing Kate's work. He purchased the copyright of her books when Edmund Evans retired in the 1890s and reissued them around 1900. This coincided with a flurry of merchandise bearing Greenaway designs on both sides of the Atlantic. The one encouraged the other. Not until organized sales promotions in the late twentieth century has anyone been able to rival the international acclaim accorded the Greenaway style. Kate regularly received requests for interviews, photographs, locks of hair and other memorabilia from abroad.

As early as 1883 she was approached to lend her name to the design of a child's shoe. She refused, feeling this would devalue her art and, since feet were a part of the anatomy she had endless problems drawing, she had no wish to focus attention on them. Whether she granted her permission or not, goods were offered for sale using her designs, even her name, and she was powerless to prevent or profit from this exploitation.

The first Greenaway copies appeared within weeks of the publication of *Under The Window*. Kate was upset. She considered *Afternoon Tea: a book of new rhymes for children* by J G Sowerby and H H Emmerson to be blatant piracy. Edmund Evans was furious: 'Of course I could have nothing to do with such a bare-faced copy of K.G.'s book,' he wrote angrily in his reminiscences. 'It was, of course, bought and published by another firm of publishers and soon got classed among the "Kate Greenaway Books" which flooded the booksellers' shops for years to follow.'[2] Sowerby argued that his designs were simply in the same genre as Greenaway's and Crane's and not in imitation.

The line between plagiarizing and working in a similar style is hard to define. Betweeen 1880 and 1882 Royal Worcester produced some delicate porcelain figures which, in their high-waisted frocks and buttoned-up trews, looked remarkably like Greenaway children. They described these figures as 'Queen Anne', a term much used for designs after the Aesthetic fashion. The porcelain was tinted and gilded for the American market but left as plain ivory for the English dining-table. Holes were pierced in the top of the boys' beaver hats or girls' bonnets so that the figures could be used as sugar sifters. The company's pattern books show that their principal designer, James Hadley, created many variations of these Greenaway children. Some formed large table decorations, comprising several figures and sections of rustic fencing, which the

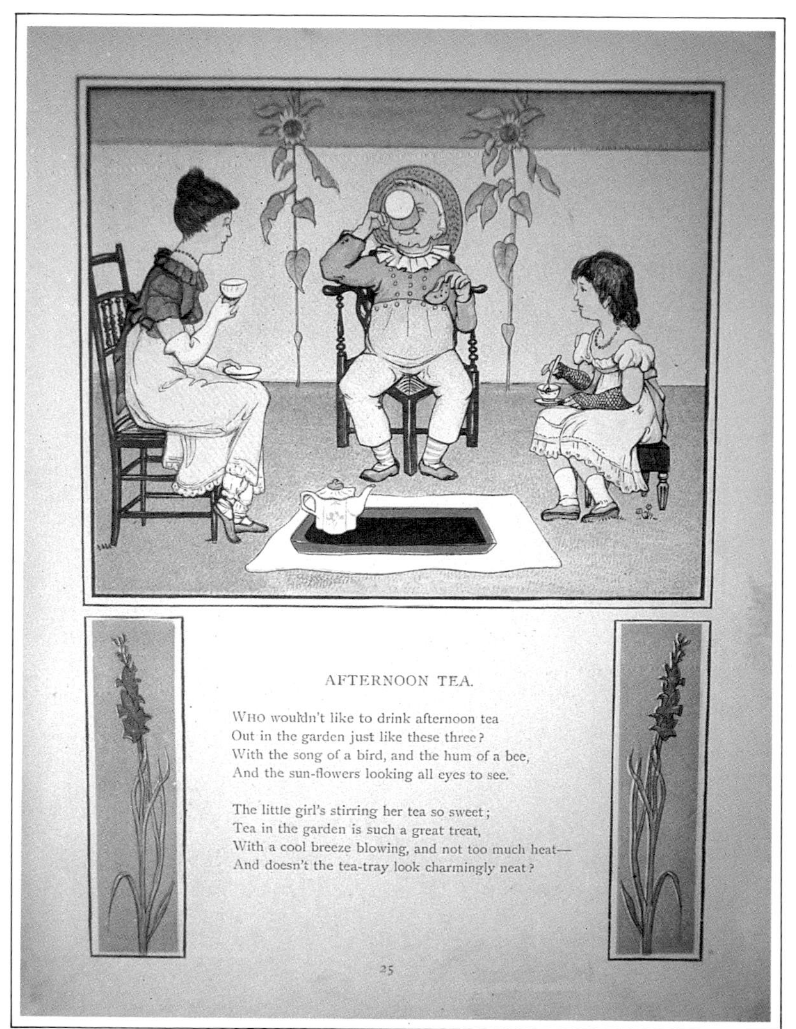

AFTERNOON TEA.

WHO wouldn't like to drink afternoon tea
Out in the garden just like these three?
With the song of a bird, and the hum of a bee,
And the sun-flowers looking all eyes to see.

The little girl's stirring her tea so sweet;
Tea in the garden is such a great treat,
With a cool breeze blowing, and not too much heat—
And doesn't the tea-tray look charmingly neat?

25

A page from Sowerby and Emmerson's book AFTERNOON TEA *published only months after Kate's bestselling* UNDER THE WINDOW. *Although the authors argued that it was not an imitation, the costumes, china, sunflowers, indeed the whole page layout bear a marked similarity to the Greenaway book. The execution of the figures is, however, far inferior, as the leg of the left-hand girl shows.*

The central design on one of Royal Doulton's 'Almanack' plates which uses an illustration from Kate's original ALMANACK *books.*

Above:
Two of the very fine Greenaway-style figures modelled by the 'art potter' James Hadley for the Royal Worcester Porcelain Company in 1882. These are now extremely rare.

Opposite:
In this calendar for 1899, Kate has dressed each girl to represent one of the twelve months. The idea was adapted for a wallpaper design.

hostess could arrange as she wished. Other single figures supported baskets which could hold candelabra, small fountains or containers for flowers.

The Royal Worcester Porcelain Company also produced a range of figures as candle extinguishers. Amongst these were an oriental gentleman, characters from contemporary court cases and, in 1881, a Greenaway baby with a large feathered hat and ornate beribboned dress as well as a Greenaway girl dressed for a party with frills and fan.

In 1882 Hadley made two pairs of small hand-painted Greenaway children. These figures are now extremely rare. Pictured above are two of the little girls from the sets, the boys who once sat astride chairs having disappeared. The ornaments would have been expensive at the time of their manufacture and were probably sold through Royal Worcester's showroom in New Bond Street or through Liberty's in London. It is clear that Hadley had his finger carefully on the pulse of fashion because he ceased modelling Greenaway children in 1883.

When the interest in Greenaway moved to a popular level, cheaper porcelain figures appeared from the Continent towards the end of the century. Sometimes these were transfer-printed, or hand-coloured, or left in white hard-paste porcelain.

In the 1890s Greenaway designs also began appearing on tiles. Unlike Walter Crane, Kate never acted as a designer for any tile

Kate Greenaway's Calendar for 1899.
ENGRAVED AND PRINTED BY
EDMUND EVANS
RACQUET COURT, FLEET STREET, E.C.

A tile 'after Greenaway' manufactured by the Shropshire firm of Craven Dunnill in their series 'Children's Games'. This particular tile was discovered in bits in the debris of the factory during recent excavations.

company nor did she license them to reproduce her work. Nevertheless, plenty of Greenaway-style tiles appeared and have since become attributed to her. Tiles such as the blue and white skipping scene above, which forms part of a series of children's games produced by the famous tilemaker Craven Dunnill in Shropshire, were sold for nursery use.

Wallpaper was one of the few items Kate officially sanctioned. In 1893 she sold the original artwork for one of her *Almanacks* to David Walker & Co of Middleton, with permission for them to reproduce a 'sanitary wall-paper' for the nursery. The finished paper contained a frieze of the seasons at the top and featured the different months of the year in the main body. Several other Greenaway wallpapers appeared around the turn of the century but it is doubtful whether they had Kate's blessing.

For the occupants of the nursery there have always been the original Kate Greenaway books. First editions of these are much prized and Schuster and Engen's *Printed Kate Greenaway: A Catalogue Raisonné* provides an excellent guide to the numerous bindings and different editions which appeared. Many of Kate's books continue in print but few modern editions can match the clarity of colour which Edmund Evans achieved with his inks and wood blocks.

There were not only Greenaway books to amuse the children but also Greenaway toys. The beautiful bone china dolls' tea-set shown opposite was made by Grimwade Ltd of Stoke-on-Trent around 1913. Given the exceptionally fine quality of this particular tea-service it is questionable whether it was really intended for children.

Similarly the Greenaway dolls which have survived from this period suggest careful adult owners rather than children. Many dolls seem to have been dressed by individuals in imitation of either a character in a Greenaway book or one on a Christmas card. The doll shown on page 117 has a papier mâché head, arms and legs. She is thought to have been made in Germany in the 1890s. Not all the Greenaway dolls made at the turn of the century were of papier mâché. Some were made of china, while a cut-out cloth Greenaway doll was advertised in America by the Saalfield Publishing Company in 1914 and cut-out paper dolls with sets of clothes, and suitable Greenaway names like 'Polly Prim', were also on sale in the United States. In recent years there has been a revival of interest in Greenaway dolls, and Royal Doulton manufactured a limited edition of Kate Greenaway dolls with china heads and hands in the 1980s.

In America even more than in England, the Greenaway image flourished. Kate's illustrations were pirated mercilessly during her lifetime. Despite the problems of distance and communication in late-Victorian times, the American market never lagged behind the

Part of a fine bone china dolls' tea-set made around 1913 by the Stoke-on-Trent firm of Grimwade. Kate never sanctioned the use of her designs for such items and was powerless to stop them.

English one; if anything it led the way. As early as 1877 there appeared a *Baby's Own Primer* illicitly using Kate's illustrations, and throughout the 1880s and 1890s there appeared a steady stream of Greenaway books, both authorized and unauthorized. American publishers generally stopped short of reissuing her books, largely because there were official editions already in existence, but many of her drawings were used illicitly to decorate different selections of nursery rhymes or anthologies of children's stories, causing one publisher cheekily to advertise his books as 'beautifully illustrated'. A New York publisher commissioned one of his artists to copy the drawings in *Under The Window* and put in slight variations, then he reissued the book in parts with a different title and described it as 'After Kate Greenaway'. More commonly Kate's early black and white work for magazines like *Little Folks* or *The Illustrated London News* found its way back into print in America, if not to illustrate someone else's nursery stories, then as outlines in publications like *The Little Folks Painting Book.*

Kate Greenaway was recognized as big business and designs

Royal Doulton currently produces this series of Kate Greenaway figures.

taken from her books were freely adapted to decorate almost anything: dance and concert programmes, menu cards, calling cards, sheet music and stationery all displayed her characteristic children.

Kate's designs were printed on fabrics as well as paper. In 1907 an American publisher produced one of Kate's alphabet books in colour, printed on muslin. Since then, curtain materials, handkerchiefs and doilies featuring Greenaway pictures have appeared steadily on both sides of the Atlantic.

Liberty's shops in London and Paris produced an elaborate range of children's clothing they called 'Kate Greenaway'. Their catalogues from 1902 until 1912 contained a section of 'Picturesque and Fashionable Dress' in which four to eight year olds could select items like a Greenaway Red Riding Hood cloak in cloth, lined with satin, for eighteen shillings and sixpence; or a typical Greenaway white muslin frock with a frill at the neck and hem, a matching muslin mob cap and silk sash for two pounds, twelve shillings and sixpence; whilst little boys could wear Greenaway suits in pink with large white ruffles at the neck and cuffs, blue socks and a white beaver hat with green band for three pounds, thirteen shillings and sixpence.

These clothes were never designed by Kate herself, merely inspired by her work, but one dress which was designed by her has survived. This was commissioned by John Ruskin in 1887 to be worn by the May Queen at Whitelands College, a training college for women teachers in Chelsea. Kate was asked to create a dress suitable for a girl of any size, since the May Queen was not elected until the morning of 1 May. Kate responded with a simple smock of cream cashmere with bands of pansies embroidered around the neck, sleeves and hem. This was worn over a moss-green silk underskirt and fastened around the waist with a green silk sash.

The essential simplicity of Kate's art has meant that it reproduces well in needlework. Even in 1882 the keen English or American needlewoman could purchase embroidery transfers for

One of the numerous Continental imports of Greenaway memorabilia. This mug, dating from the end of the nineteenth century, is of German origin.

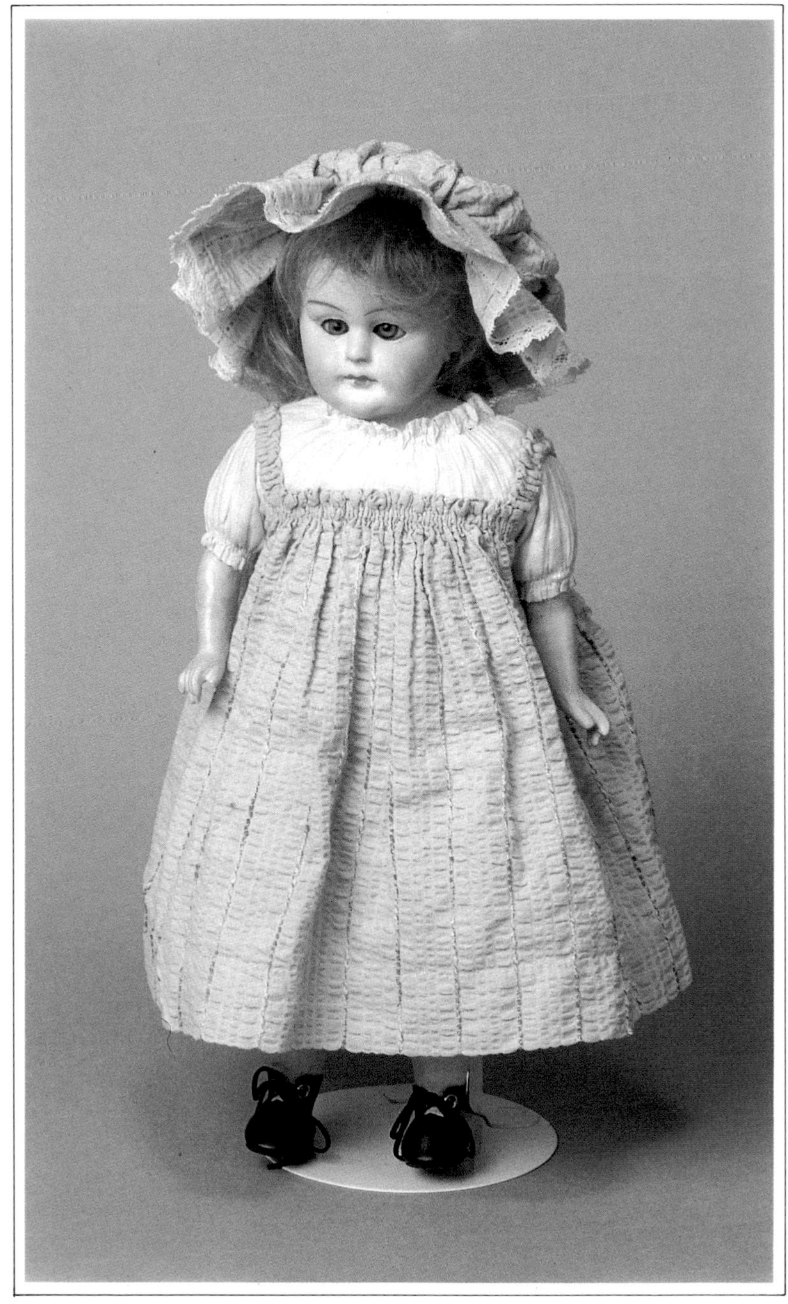

Right:
A Kate Greenaway doll thought to have been made in the 1890s in Germany for the English market. She has a papier mâché head, arms and legs and is dressed in the original clothes.

LONDON, 56 PATERNOSTER ROW

Opposite:
Kate was introduced to the subject of May Day celebrations by John Ruskin, then involved in setting them up at Whitelands College, Chelsea. This frontispiece for THE GIRL'S OWN ANNUAL *was published in 1890.*

Above:
'THE MAY DANCE', dated 1884, was originally painted as a gift for Ruskin who went on to give it to Whitelands College, Chelsea, where he had inaugurated May Day festivities. The picture was exhibited at the Fine Art Society in 1898.

The dress Kate Greenaway designed at Ruskin's request in 1887 to be worn by the May Queens at Whitelands College in London. It is a cashmere smock embroidered with a border of pansies; the underskirt of moss-green silk was to show below the smock. Seen also in this picture is the gold Hawthorn cross designed by Arthur Severn and presented on behalf of John Ruskin to the girl student chosen as May Queen that year. In 1896 Ruskin asked Kate to present the cross on his behalf.

The May Queen at Whitelands College, Chelsea, surrounded by her attendants. She is wearing the Greenaway dress.

Opposite:
In 1885 Kate published her own illustrations to that standard reading primer THE ENGLISH SPELLING BOOK *by William Mavor. The charming Greenaway children playing around each letter have often been reproduced and here they are seen on a modern embroidery sampler.*

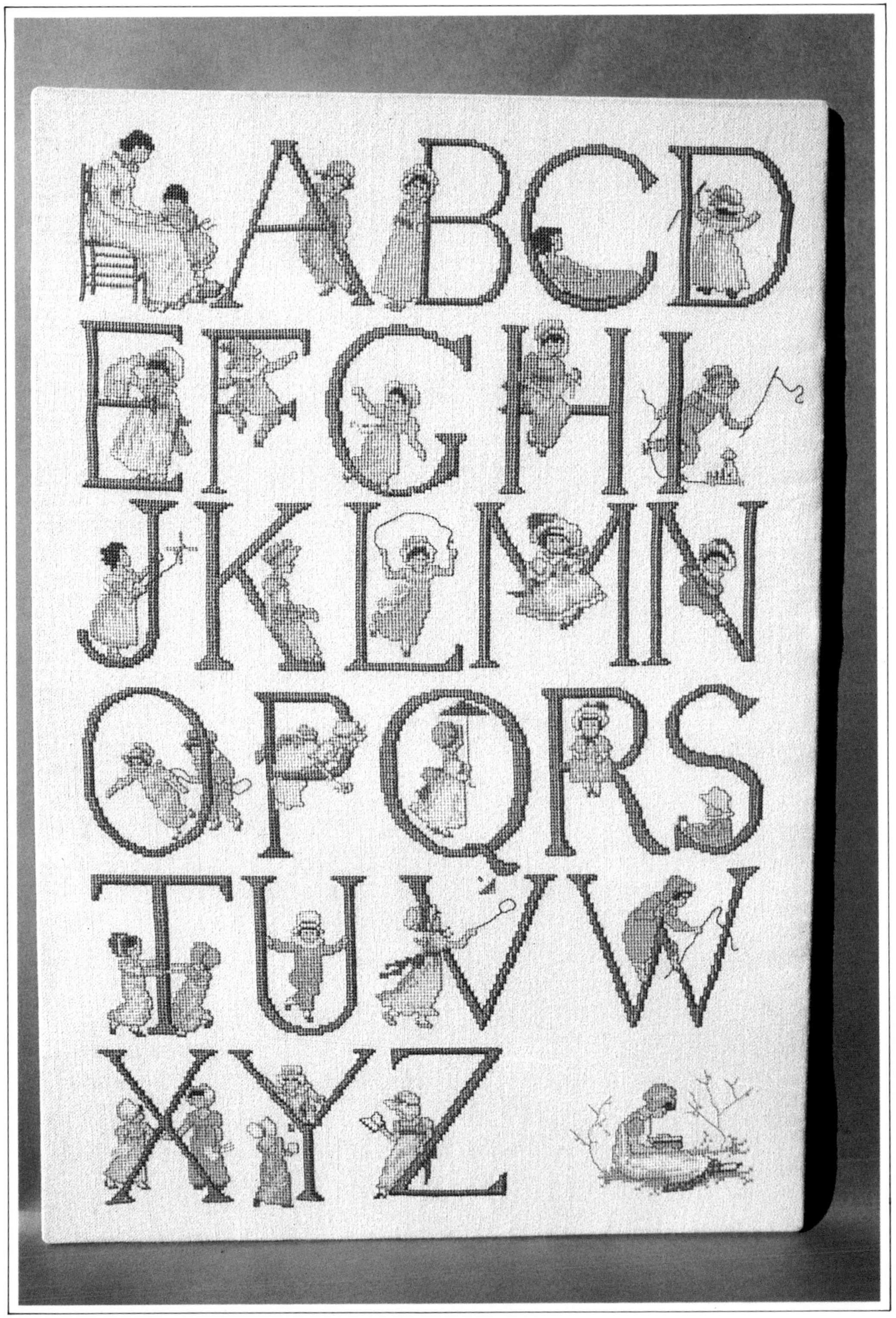

ABCD
EFGHI
JKLMN
OPQRS
TUVW
XYZ

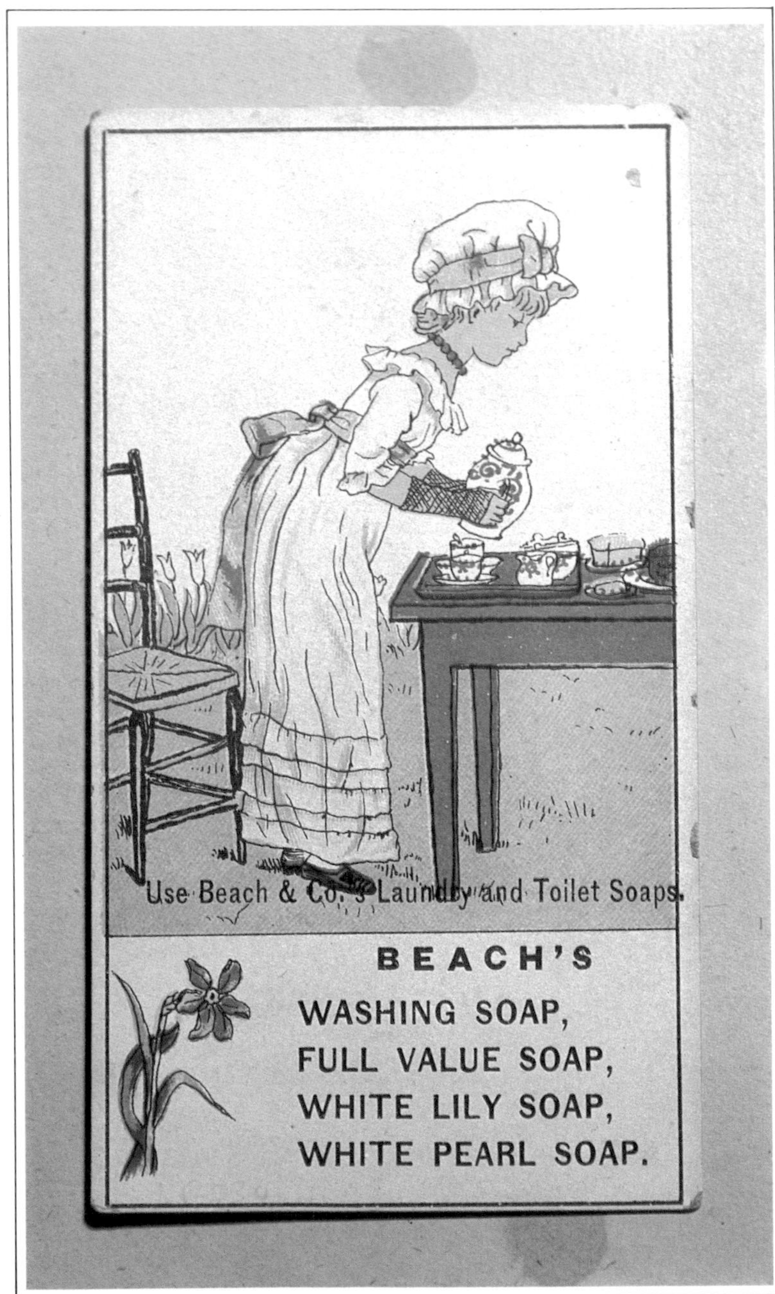

This crude imitation of a procession of Greenaway girls was used to advertise Fry's chocolate at the beginning of the century.

Left:
Once she became famous, Kate found herself exploited mercilessly. This advertisement for Beach's soap illicitly used half of a picture from UNDER THE WINDOW.

Opposite:
Kate composed the verses to KATE GREENAWAY'S CAROLS *which were published on card in 1883 by George Routledge. These cards are now much sought after by collectors.*

STARS in the sky above,
Stars in the grass below;
What happy children we,
As we merrily dance a-row!
OH, what is sweeter than little faces,
Soft blue eyes, and baby graces!
While a round red sun above us lingers,
And hands are clasped by baby fingers.
KATE GREENAWAY'S CAROLS
PINK are our Summer roses,
Youth is a happy boon;
And merry's the song we sing
As we look at the yellow moon.
AS we slowly walk along,
We would also raise our song;
Thanks for all our bygone bliss,
And the quiet peace of this.
GEORGE ROUTLEDGE & SONS, LONDON AND NEW YORK.
(Copyright.)

Kate Greenaway scenes, and pattern books for embroidering Greenaway children on to household linen like tablecloths and antimacassars date from this time. Kate has continued to inspire embroidery up to the present day, as the cross-stitch alphabet sampler on page 121 from Mavor's *The English Spelling Book*, which uses Kate's decorated initials, demonstrates.

It is possible to collect Kate Greenaway designs on almost any object but amongst the more interesting and unusual nineteenth-century memorabilia are buttons. They were generally made of metal, marked 'TW & W', 'HM' and 'Paris Brevete' on the back and frequently depicted figures from *Under The Window*.

Since the Greenaway style was so recognizable and popular it was used on many early advertisements. The crude imitation of Greenaway girls on page 122 (right) was used to advertise Fry's chocolate. Trade cards, like the one on page 122 (left) advertising Beach's toilet and laundry soap, also made free with Kate's work, in this case just the left half of a picture from *Under The Window*.

A hundred years on, interest in Kate Greenaway memorabilia shows no sign of abating and the Greenaway industry has proved to be the forerunner of modern merchandizing. Kate, sadly, received little financial gain from the goods that bore her designs. Because of them however her name and art have been accorded a renown they might not otherwise have gained in spite of the beauty and timeless quality of her work.

REFERENCES

1 Letter from Kate Greenaway to John Ruskin 27 May 1898
2 McLean p61

Lilies were amongst Kate's favourite flowers, not only on account of their shape but also their scent. She planted large numbers in her garden and they appear in the background of many of her watercolours. This painting was in preparation for an illustration in A DAY IN A CHILD'S LIFE.

BIBLIOGRAPHY

Aslin, Elizabeth *The Aesthetic Movement: Prelude to the Art Nouveau* (Ferndale 1981)
Austwick, J and B *The Decorated Tile* (Pitman 1980)
Birkenhead, Sheila *Illustrious Friends: The Story of Joseph Severn and his son Arthur* (Hamish Hamilton 1965)
Birrell, Augustine *Frederick Locker-Lampson: A Character Sketch* (Constable 1920)
Bolton Art Gallery *Exhibition Catalogue* (Jan 1976)
Crane, Walter *An Artist's Reminiscences* (Methuen 1907)
Engen, Rodney *Kate Greenaway; a Biography* (Macdonald 1981)
Furniss, Harry *Some Victorian Women; Good, Bad and Indifferent* (John Lane, The Bodley Head 1923)
Hunt Institute, Pittsburgh *Kate Greenaway: A Catalog* (1980)
Locker-Lampson, Frederick *London Lyrics* (Macmillan 1904)
Locker-Lampson, Frederick *My Confidences* (Thomas Nelson and Smith Elder 1895)
McLean, Ruari (ed) *The Reminiscences of Edmund Evans* (Oxford 1967)
Nevill, Ralph (ed) *The Reminiscences of Lady Dorothy Nevill* (Arnold 1907)
Petersons, Margaret *The Rowfant Story* (Rowfant House 1980)
Reynolds, Jan *Birket Foster* (Batsford 1984)
Saint, Andrew *Richard Norman Shaw* (Yale University Press 1976)
Schuster, T E and Engen, Rodney *Printed Kate Greenaway: A Catalogue Raisonné* (T E Schuster 1986)
Spielmann, M H and Layard, G S *The Life and Works of Kate Greenaway* (A & C Black 1905)
Viljoen, Helen Gill (ed) *The Brantwood Diary of John Ruskin* (Yale University Press 1971)
Whitelands College, Chelsea, London *Annuals*

MAGAZINES
Anon 'Art in the Nursery' *Magazine of Art* 1883 vol 6 pp127–32
Dobson, Austin 'Kate Greenaway' *Art Journal* Feb 1902 pp33–6 and 105–9
Locker-Lampson, Oliver 'Kate Greenaway, Friend of Children' *Century Magazine* vol LXXV Dec 1907 pp183–94
Spielmann, M H 'Kate Greenaway: In Memoriam' *Magazine of Art* 1902 pp118–22
A Student Friend 'Reminiscences of Kate Greenaway in Hampstead' *Hampstead Annals* 1906–7 pp100–8
White, Gleeson 'Children's Books and their Illustrators' *Studio* Extra Christmas Number 1897–8
White, Gleeson 'Christmas Cards and their Chief Designers' *Studio* Extra Christmas Number 1894

UNPUBLISHED
Kate Greenaway's Memoirs and Letters in Special Collections of the University Libraries of Carnegie Mellon University, Pittsburgh, USA

ACKNOWLEDGEMENTS

I have been most grateful for the assistance of many people in researching Kate Greenaway's life and art but would especially like to thank the following:

Mr and Mrs B Austwick; Mr and Mrs Guy Azis; Mr Nick Azis; Ms Janet Barnes; Mrs Jennifer Carter; Mrs Helen Cocker; Mr Malcolm Cole; Mrs Wendy Cook; Mr Roger Cucksey; the late Mrs J A Davico; Miss Roberta Davis; Mr James Dearden; Ms Lesley Durban; Mrs G E Fairhurst; Mr Peter Fennymore; Mrs Christina Gee; Miss Annie Goodenough; the late Mrs Kathleen Goldsack; Mr Dean Gosbee; Mr Michael Heseltine; Mr Bruce Irving; Ms Patricia Ivinski; Ms Mary Catharine Johnsen; Mr Jeremy Maas; Mr Frank Mitchell; Mrs Lucy Paul; Mrs Margaret Petersons; The Hon Miss Laura Ponsonby; Mr H Ratcliffe; Miss Jan Reynolds; Dr Catherine Ross; Mrs Elizabeth Rumbelow; Mrs Gina Stead; Mr Robert Taylor; Mrs Ada Whittingham.

I should also like to express my thanks to Annabel Watts, who assisted me with the research; Marianne Morris who took many of the photographs and my husband Colin whose editorial skills were as always greatly appreciated.

The following have also assisted with my research and I should like to record my thanks:

Abbot Hall Art Gallery, Cumbria; Ashmolean Museum, Oxford; Bethnal Green Museum of Childhood, London; Birmingham Central Reference Library; The British Library, London; Bucentaur Gallery Ltd; Special Collections of the Carnegie Mellon University, Pittsburgh; Castle Howard Archives, York; Christie's New York; County Reference Library and County Record Office, Isle of Wight; Crawley Library, Sussex; De Grummond Collection, University of Southern Mississippi; Delaware Art Museum; Dyson Perrins Museum Trust, Worcester; Fine Art Society, London; Gladstone Pottery Museum, Staffordshire; Graves Art Gallery, Sheffield; Mary Hare Grammar School; Richard Hagen Fine Paintings, Broadway; Harris Museum and Art Gallery, Preston; Huntington Library and Art Gallery, California; Islington Public Library; Jackfield Tile Museum, Ironbridge Gorge Museum Trust, Shropshire; Ivor Poole Collection, University of Illinois Library; Keats House and Camden Public Libraries, London; Laing Art Gallery, Newcastle upon Tyne; Liberty's Archive at Westminster City Archive; Local Studies, Central Library, Nottingham; Maas Gallery; Manchester City Art Gallery; National Portrait Gallery, London; Newark Museum, Nottinghamshire; Newport Museum and Art Gallery; Osborne Collection, Toronto Public Libraries, Ontario; Pierpont Morgan Library, New York; Royal Collection, Windsor Castle; Royal Academy of Arts; Royal Albert Memorial Museum, Exeter; Ruskin Gallery collection of the Guild of St George, Sheffield; Ruskin Gallery, Bembridge School, Isle of Wight; John Rylands Library, Manchester; Sotheby's, Belgravia; Henry Sotheran Ltd; Special Collections Library, University of California; Sterling and Francine Clark Art Institute, Massachusetts; Swiss Cottage Library, London; Tennyson Research Centre, Central Reference Library, Lincoln; Towneley Hall Art Gallery and Museum, Burnley; Ulster Museum; Victoria and Albert Museum, London; Walker Art Gallery, Liverpool; Walsall Art Gallery; Wedgwood Museum, Staffordshire; Whitelands College Archives, London; Witt Library, Courtauld Institute Galleries, London.

PICTURE CREDITS

The author and publishers wish to thank the following for supplying illustrations: pages 9, 10, 17 right, 19 left, 20, 28 above left, 32, 33, 35 left, 37, 38, 39, 40, 42, 43, 44, 47, 52 above, 73 above, 75, 77, 80, 98 centre, 113, 122 left and 123 are reproduced by permission of the London Borough of Camden from the Collections at Keats House, Hampstead; pages 11 left, 18 above, 19 right, 22 left, 22 below right, 24 right, 28 below left, 28 right, 41 left, 48 left, 51, 53 right, 55, 70, 76, 83, 84 left, 88, 100 lower, 102 left, 104, 105 and 118 are by kind permission of Annabel Watts; page 81 is by kind permission of the Ruskin Gallery, Collection of the Guild of St George, Sheffield; pages 12, 41 right and 84 right are by courtesy of Sotheby's, London; page 78 is by permission of the Ruskin Gallery, Bembridge School, Isle of Wight; page 96 is reproduced from Marley plc's collection of original Helen Allingham watercolours; pages 14, 50, 54, 63, 79, 86, 94, 97, 98 left, 99, 101, 102 right and 124 are reproduced from the Special Collections of the Carnegie Mellon University, Pittsburgh, Pennsylvania, USA; pages 18 below, 43 left, 85 and 98 right are by courtesy of the Sterling and Francine Clark Art Institute, Williamstown, Massachusetts, USA; page 21 is by permission of the Maas Gallery and has been reproduced as a greetings card by The Bucentaur Gallery Ltd; pages 22 above right and 35 centre are by kind permission of Richard Hagen Fine Paintings, Broadway, Worcestershire; pages 34 and 35 right are by courtesy of the Ulster Museum and Art Gallery, Belfast; page 103 is from the collection of the Harris Museum and Art Gallery, Preston; page 46 is reproduced by kind permission of Jan Reynolds and William Glasson; pages 53 left, 73 below and 95 are reproduced by permission of the National Portrait Gallery, London; page 60 is by kind permission of Mrs G Fairhurst; page 61 is by courtesy of the Trustees of the National Museums and Galleries on Merseyside (Walker Art Gallery, Liverpool); page 72 is reproduced by kind permission of Mrs Ada Whittingham; page 82 is by courtesy of the Ashmolean Museum, Oxford; pages 108 and 112 are by permission of the Dyson Perrins Museum Trust at Royal Worcester; pages 111 right and 116 are by permission of Royal Doulton Ltd; page 114 is courtesy of the Jackfield Tile Museum, Ironbridge Gorge Museum Trust; page 115 is kindly reproduced from The Wait Teapot Collection, Newport Museum and Art Gallery, Gwent; page 117 is by kind permission of Mrs Jennifer Carter; pages 119 and 120 are by courtesy of Whitelands College Archives, London. Other illustrations are from the author's collection.

INDEX

Page numbers in *italics* refer to captions and pictures.